WENDY JONES is the author of the bestselling biography of Grayson Perry, *Portrait of the Artist as a Young Girl*. She writes the Wilfred Price novels: *The Thoughts and Happenings of Wilfred Price, Purveyor of Superior Funerals* and *The World is a Wedding*. She also writes for television.

Wendy Jones has a PhD from Goldsmiths in Creative Writing and the books of Studs Terkel, and was the first person to do the MA in Life Writing at the University of East Anglia. She lives in London.

D0183901

# THE
# SEX LIVES
# OF
# ENGLISH
# WOMEN

*Intimate Questions
and Unexpected
Answers*

## WENDY JONES

**For women**

# Contents

# Some thoughts

This book is not about how to be a woman; it is about how women are. Women are always being told how to be a woman: how to be sexy/thin/fashionable/beautiful/attractive to men, how to organise a perfect wedding/decorate/cook/lose weight/ dress, how to be pregnant/give birth/mother, what jobs they can do, what rape is, how to stop ageing, what colour powder to put on their eyelids, how to have good self-esteem. And so on. There is so much telling women how they should be, and so little asking them who they are and what they want. I thought someone should at least have the courtesy to ask.

This is a book of interviews with twenty-four English women talking about sex. When I began, I had no agenda, I wanted to listen to women, to give women the space to speak. And I wanted to interview English women, who so often have a reputation for being sexually repressed. I had two questions: what is it to be a woman? and, what do women want sexually? This book is my answer.

I found the women in various ways. Shirley, a feminist in

her seventies, sat next to me on the train; the Muslim teenager served me in the supermarket; a friend of a friend suggested interviewing Mary, the 94-year-old. I met Hilary, the Girl Guides leader, at a conference on domestic violence; I went to a burlesque class to find Samantha. I turned to social media, and women came forward. If I had an instinct about someone, I asked, and she invariably said yes.

I wanted experiences and stories. I didn't want statistics – such as that the average act of intercourse has three hundred thrusts, true though that may be. I didn't want to reduce women to facts and figures about orgiastic spasms, orgiastic discharges and so on: that seemed dehumanising and I was in search of the women's humanity and individuality. I wagered that through our sexuality our humanity is revealed. All names, identifying details and places, have been changed to protect the women's anonymity. Every woman had right of veto.

From my own experience I was able to understand a lot of what the women were saying. Yet, as a heterosexual woman, I didn't know other women the way an average heterosexual man – or gay or bisexual woman – would: from sleeping with them. I knew women and didn't know them. I wanted to reveal what was hidden.

The women had a lot to say – the unedited interviews came to half a million words. Beneath the armour of respectability, behind closed doors, women are full of it. When women talk about sex they talk about their bodies and their vaginas. Paula describes her vagina as fat. Gwyn's job is massaging vaginas. Mary's vagina was surgically constructed from the skin of her penis. And they talk about orgasms. Victoria describes having seven or eight in one session, Deborah, forty-one, thinks she's never had one. Helen describes womb orgasms, Pandora, a trapeze artist, likes to scream.

I was curious about women's fantasies. In fantasy, unlike in reality, there is absolute freedom. What does a woman want if you take out the restraints of monogamy, marriage, age, health, religion, social mores, and financial strictures? What does a woman choose to do when she can desire anything? May imagines the sea as her lover. Sigourney, a shop assistant, wants a threesome. Pandora wouldn't mind having her own harem. Ariel, a beauty contestant, fantasised about sex in a hot tub – so she had it. But women don't always want their fantasies to come true. Christina didn't want to be raped, despite her fantasy; Farah would like to do vampire stuff, but didn't want to be bitten too hard on her neck. There can be a gap between what a woman desires in her mind and what she wants in her life.

I had thought some women would know a lot about sex and some wouldn't. But it was more complex than that. Yvette had four children before she knew what her own vagina looked like. Charlotte, the gynaecological nurse, didn't know what an orgasm was. And Jackie, despite having slept with ten men a day, was scared to hold a man's hand. I saw it again and again in the interviews: that slice of rich experience and that space of innocence. They are interviews of innocence and experience. The sharp distinction between the virgin and the whore came to seem wholly artificial – another false construct to try to shove women into, like poorly fitted and contorting shoes.

When women talk about sex they talk about religion. Their parents' – even their ancestors' – religion and its coercive bonds often echo in their own life, decades later. Yet, if sex is not a sin any more, it is often a source of anxiety. There is a sense of unease around pornography, and differing viewpoints. While Lois is illuminated by porn, Lola, twenty-three, feels sad after she's watched it. Because of porn, Farah's boyfriend wants her clean-shaven. Olive first watched porn when she was a nun. And women mentioned difficult sexual experiences in many interviews. Caused not only by men, but by chance, by genetics, by other children, by mothers, by family, by society. There is a sadism in our society towards female sexuality. Sometimes a woman's sexuality is a decimated landscape. Yet women survive and are full of power and life force. English women don't lie back. They don't think of England.

When women talk about good sex they say 'yes' a lot. James Joyce described yes as 'the female word', and many 'yeses' lace their way through these conversations. 'Yes' is the nearest women have to express their deepest joy, the only word left when all others fail to express what she is feeling. It is the word of the sexually happy woman. Look out for the yeses.

Thirty-two thousand years ago, men and women painted a cave in Chauvet, France, and in the middle of the cave they painted a woman's pudendum. The first humans understood that female sexuality is central to life and its creation and they honoured that in a seemingly guiltless and open way. Through writing this book I came to see the wisdom and beauty of this ancient perception from the beginning of human consciousness; that female sexuality is an intense and vital force at the centre of human experience – then and now – and that through our sexuality our humanity is revealed.

Women have borne the brunt of sexual repression. But all women have the ability to express themselves sexually. Every woman has a unique sexuality and a unique story to tell about her sexuality. If I were a man, I would be in awe of women. There is more to say. Here are the interviews.

# 1

# Burlesque

Samantha, 28, Newcastle

*'I was like, "Can't believe I'm going to get on
that stage and take my clothes off"'*

'Burlesque is the art of striptease. It's very, very glamorous
and flashy. My act is classic showgirl burlesque, I have sequins
and rhinestones and a feather fan. I dance on stage and then
remove clothing to music until I'm in nipple tassels and a
thong. It's a reveal at the end for five seconds for the audience
to see me and then I leave.

The nipple tassels need to cover my areola. I use double-
sided sticky tape, which hurts. I can't moisturise before I go
on stage because the moisturiser makes the tassels slip off!
In the summer when it gets *really* hot in the venues, they're
just not going to stay on. All the girls are like, 'I don't know
what I'm going to do.' Everyone's got tips, like using hairspray,
and pressing their boobs first before they put the tassels on.
There's so many tips it's hilarious! There's wig glue that you

use to stick your wig down with. One girl uses dribble. One girl uses carpet tape, she's like, 'This does not come off.' But I wouldn't want to use it. It's funny.

I do burlesque in clubs all over London and theatre tours in huge theatres. It doesn't ever feel like a job at all. All the women I work with are the most amazing, intelligent, strong, confident, fantastic women, and everyone is so lovely to each other. There's a real sense of community among burlesque dancers so if there's a dodgy photographer or a dodgy promoter, everybody will message, 'Watch out for this guy, don't reply to him.' We look out for each other. Most of the girls are English. Average age is probably mid to late twenties, early thirties. There's not that many younger ones; people find it a little bit uncomfortable when the girls are too young. There was one girl and she was seventeen. I know at seventeen you think you're a woman. That's a little bit too young to be doing a show; you haven't really had enough experience. I hadn't even had sex when I was seventeen so I wouldn't have been able to dance how I dance because I wouldn't have known how to do it. If you're young you don't really get that same rapport with an audience.

When I went to dance college at eighteen the main thing with me was always, 'Yeah, you're very good, you're very talented. You need to be taller, you need to lose weight.' I can't be taller. So it was always, 'If you're going to be short' – which I am – 'you need to be tiny.' I was under so much pressure all the time to lose weight. Some of my teachers – they were lovely, and they were doing it for my own good – but they thought I wasn't trying hard enough, or I was eating what I wanted. I'm just naturally *not* a size 6, or a size 8. It did get a bit on top of me, and in the last year of college I was *not* eating anything. I was eating a side salad a day, I was taking these diet pills that I got off the Internet. And I lost *so* much weight. And they were like, 'You look amazing!' but I was *so* unhappy. I couldn't dance like I wanted to dance; I had no energy. I never got an eating disorder because I was doing it to be thin; it wasn't a mental thing. As soon as I left college I was like, 'I can't do this, I can't starve myself.' I moved to London, went to a burlesque night. I watched these girls and I was like, 'I can definitely do that because I can dance already, and I don't need to starve myself.' My friends were like, 'Yeah, go for it, you'll be so good at that.'

The first time I was like, 'Can't believe I'm going to get on that stage and take my clothes off.' I was terrified. But I've always been a bit of an exhibitionist. Despite being told all the time I need to lose weight, I've never had any hang-ups about my body. I was really nervous, but in a *good* way. As soon as I'd done it I absolutely *loved* it and I was like, I'm just going to go for this. Like anything in life there's a certain level of fate, and things started coming my way to do with burlesque. I was like, yeah, this is obviously the right path for now. It's been five years, so it accidentally became a career!

There's a lot of different types of burlesque: you have comedy burlesque, classic burlesque – which is all the feathers, Twenties burlesque, which is the older style, then there's neo-burlesque where there's tattooed girls with piercings. With burlesque, it's about the performance. It's not like modelling where you have to look a certain way. I've seen girls who are a good size 16 come on that stage and *absolutely* kill, and the audience are going *wild*. One girl's eighteen stone. It challenges people's ideas of what is aesthetically pleasing. I think that's why people love it so much.

I get so many lovely compliments from women saying it's nice to see somebody on stage who's got curves, who isn't stick-thin and who isn't ashamed of it or embarrassed. The amount of women that stop me afterwards and say, 'It's nice to see someone with a normal body.' Sometimes the word 'normal' annoys me because I think, 'Well, what is normal? Everyone's different.' Or they'll say, 'It's nice to see a real woman.' That term annoys me because thin women aren't imaginary, they're still real. I had a bad experience once, where somebody said I had cellulite! I just couldn't stop laughing, I was, 'Yup, I do! So do most people!'

It's titillating, but it's not in the same way that a stripper would be. Sometimes people are getting turned on. I don't know if that's because on that night I'm a bit drunk! And I'm feeling a bit sexier. I've had people go afterwards, 'Oh my God, that was amazing, I think I fancy you.' Sometimes I get turned on, very rarely. Most of the time I go into autopilot. If there's someone in the audience I lock eyes with or I think's pretty hot, then I would get turned on, yeah. Young men come, but not very often. I'd say the men are late twenties, early thirties. Not that young. The older men, they're definitely the pervier ones! The groups of City workers who are in their forties and fifties can get a bit leery when I'm offstage. They'll say something like, 'You don't get many of them for the pound,' about my boobs and I'm like, 'Oh, for God's sake, I haven't heard that before.' The secret with guys like that is to banter back. As soon as you get all uppity and snooty they're going to do it more. I always try and banter back and laugh.

Over Christmas I had really bad flu and I had to put make-up on and dance and it was *awful*. But it's a performance, I've got to put a smile on and suck it up. It's not the nicest thing doing burlesque when I've got my period, I am a bit aware of it. I've known a girl who came on onstage and that was *awful*. She didn't realise she was going to come on her period. Nobody

4

noticed it: obviously she did. Backstage, everyone's so past that being a taboo, 'Oh, I'm on my period, has anyone got a tampon?' I never see it as a problem massively. It's like a job; you have to get on with it.

My family's all from Newcastle. My mum's family are musical. My mum knows what I do and loves it, as does my sister. My grandma used to make my costumes but I don't think she realised *quite* what I did. And my dad I'm not really in touch with. I don't think he would mind, he's a pretty open-minded fellow, but it's not really something I would discuss with him. I tell my mum *everything*. I told my mum the first time I had sex. I've always had a really good relationship with my mum and I think for that reason I've never had any hang-ups or felt guilty for doing things. She would always say, 'Respect yourself and do things because you want to and not because you feel pressured,' and I never did anything I didn't want to do. I don't think she'd be too happy if she knew how many people I'd slept with! But I'm at a stage now, I'm like, it's my life, and you only live once. I could die tomorrow.

Sometimes I get changed and come out and have a drink afterwards but people are so lovely. People say you must get hit on, but I don't really. Men are nice. They get a bit intimidated and don't really want to speak to me. I never sleep with the people in the audience. Never have. I think, keep work separate from social life. If I have a drink after a show there's a point where I think, I should go home now. Because it has a tendency to get messy so I do like to keep my work separate from my social life. I'd be quite worried if I met someone in a club like that, I don't know what they're like or who they are, and what if they kept turning up? It would be too much of a risk. I wouldn't be able to do prostitution but I sympathise with the sex industry at lot and I think it should be legalised to protect the girls. And porn never bothers me. I'm not a very judgmental person at all.

I really got really irate about the Page 3 scandal. A lot of people – who are friends as well – are so 'Yes! They're going to end topless women on Page 3 in the *Sun* newspaper,' I thought, who are you to tell a woman she can't do that? I am really strongly feminist. For hundreds of years women have been told by men what they could and couldn't do, and now it's women telling other women what they can't do. If you don't like it, don't look at it! If people want to do that and they're making *good* money from it, let them do it. Nudity just *doesn't* offend me in *any* way. Page 3 I don't find offensive at all. I would much rather see a girl who's a good size 12 and curvy and healthy than women in women's magazines who are anorexic or starving, because that's an unrealistic image of beauty. Women seem to put this pressure on themselves to be so thin and it's really sad. It seems to be women going against other women. I think feminism's eaten itself a bit for that reason.

My job does give me a good insight into men. Men are like children. Once you know that, you know everything about them. They want what they can't have. They chase things to be stubborn. If you say, 'You can't have that, you can't do that,' they're going to want to do the opposite. Women make the mistake of thinking men are more complicated than they are, whereas I think men do what they want to do when they want to do it and they're not playing a game, they're not over-thinking, they're just doing what they want to do! It does make me a little bit sad when my friends have all these rules. One of my best friends, I love her to bits, but she's all about game playing. As soon as she meets a guy it would be like, 'Well, you can't do this until this day, and you can't send him that and can't talk about ...' And I was like, '*Why*?' I would do whatever I want to! If I want to message them I message them, if I want to have sex with them I have sex with them. That's why I don't really agree with game playing and not having sex until the third date. The way you play it isn't going to change anything. I think, be honest from the start. Honesty is *really, really* important. If you can be honest with someone and they can be honest with you, I think you've cracked it.

I've slept with lots of people. I think it's a lot. Thirty, thirty-one. Most of that was when I was travelling! I was in South America for three and a half months. It wasn't that bad; it was fourteen, maybe fifteen. Everyone's a backpacker in a hostel and everyone's having a drink and most people are single, and it's very easy to meet someone. It would be like, well, I'm having a good time with him and I want to go down to the beach, and then it just happens. I was like, it's not me, I can do what I want and this isn't usually who I am. No one can judge me because tomorrow I'll be in a different country and no one will know this happened! I never felt bad about it because I thought, it's the time of my life where I can actually do what the hell I want and no one's going to judge. That was a bit of a mad era. I've just come back. I already want to go back again.

I haven't got a boyfriend. When I went travelling I met an *amazing* English guy who lives in São Paulo, he's *lovely*, he's *amazing* but he's obviously still in São Paulo and I'm here. We're not in a relationship, we kind of are; it's complicated. My head and heart are with him but there's no way I could not have sex for that long! I could do about a month without sex and then that would be it. When I'm single I've always got a few boys and men that I have good relationships with, that I can message – 'Do you want to come over?' 'Shall I come over?' 'Do you want to go for a drink?' And then, you know ...

Actually I had a really, *really* good friend and we were sleeping together for six months. We were also best mates. None of my friends could understand it, they were like, 'Well, you're not having a relationship, you're really good friends, it's just sex?' and we were like, 'Yeah!' Both of us were completely fine with it, we could both talk about other people, there was no jealousy, there were no strings, and that was fine. That's rare, generally one person gets more attached and wants more.

Most of the time I feel sexually fulfilled. I'm a bit hedonistic. I find it really exciting when I'm with someone new for the first time. When I first start dating then sex has got to be exciting. When you start to know each other so well it becomes routine and you know what they're going to do and it's not exciting. Working at a marriage where people are monogamous must be *really* hard work. People who have been together forty years and have never cheated, I think, 'God, I don't know how they've done it'. It worries me and every time I bring this up with a friend, they say, 'Oh, it will be different when you meet the right person.' I don't know if that's true or if I'm always going to have to have an understanding with someone. If I'm with the right person they're going to have to have the same ideas on sex as me, which is open-minded. There was someone recently, he was *lovely*, but he was so boring, he didn't really stimulate my mind. The sex was very bog standard, missionary, then that would be it! For me that's not exciting at *all*. In long relationships, I get really bored of sleeping with the same person. I was with my last boyfriend for four years, and until the last year I didn't want to sleep with anyone else. He was very, very prudish and traditional in that if I ever mentioned about maybe we should have an open relationship then he would freak out.

In the bedroom I'm quite submissive, which is the complete

*opposite* of how I am in real life. In my real life I'm single and confident and I can command a room in what I do. There must be some psychology behind that. I don't know where that comes from. I like a submissive sexual relationship, just being completely dominated by somebody and having power taken away from me. Somebody telling me what to do, being tied up, anything where I've got no power and I'm giving somebody else power over me. In my real life I would hate that. It's weird! I've never done it properly. It's something I'd like to explore. One of my best friends is a dominatrix, and she's told me about club nights. I think, 'God, it is exciting,' but there's a difference between a fantasy and reality, so I don't know if it would live up to anything I've imagined or if it would be a let-down.

It's quite shameful for women to be sexually confident. Burlesque goes completely against that and says, 'No, it's fine.' Burlesque is a lovely thing for women because it puts women up there. Men worship them like a goddess. A burlesque club is definitely a woman's domain. When burlesque started during the Depression, showing a flash of knee was risqué. Knickers and nipple tassels isn't that risqué by today's standards. Nobody gets really horrified – I mean, some women do. It's forty-year-olds. Sometimes I can see them in the audience and they can be scowling and not wanting to smile. I don't know if they feel threatened. I get sad when I see couples that come to burlesque shows and the man seems like he can't even look at me or he might get told off by the woman. They must not have a very close connection. Surely she'd know that he isn't going to run off with me and I don't really care about him! That couldn't work for me. I've always been trusting with boyfriends.

When I was being told at dance college to lose weight, I

did constantly compare myself to other girls. When I started doing burlesque it gave me so much confidence because all the girls were different. I never feel embarrassed or not good enough. There's loads of things I don't like about my body. There's times where I've ate too much and think I need to lose a little bit of weight, or there are times where I'm drinking too much, but generally as long as I'm healthy – health is the most *important* thing. I always think there's someone out there wishing they had what you had. So I just be grateful for what I've got.

I absolutely love burlesque. I find it really liberating. I feel the naked body shouldn't be offensive in any way. It's something about watching a woman, who isn't a size 8 and who doesn't have a perfect body, taking her clothes off in front of all these people and not caring and enjoying herself and people sense that and find it really impressive: you endear people to you for that reason. Because you're not perfect and you don't need to be. Imperfection is what makes people beautiful. If somebody is too perfect, they lose something. Women can relate to burlesque. And men just find it sexy because it's a girl taking her clothes off. Men don't care if you're a little bit overweight. They're not as critical as women.

I never feel ashamed. Never. In the future when I look at pictures I'll never think, 'Oh God, what was I doing?' I'll think, 'Look how great I looked then! At one point in my life I looked that good!' It will be interesting in ten years' time: it will make a good story at a dinner party. 'Look what I used to do.'

## 2

# Addict

Lois, 32, London

*'Sex with a woman is different'*

'Before I got together with my girlfriend, who's my first sexual lesbian relationship, I was dating men and having sex with men – and often enjoying sex with men. The thing that I always loved about sex with men was the initial penetration. I miss penetration. I miss the way a man changes from not being aroused to being aroused: there is something spectacular about that. It's funny because I would think, 'I need it, I need it, I need it,' and after the initial penetration I was like, 'This is just the most amazing thing ever,' then I would want to stop after that. As soon as possible. I wouldn't enjoy it from about one minute in. I'd be waiting for it to be over. We might do different positions but I wasn't present any more. And that would be how sex with a man played out for me.

Sex with a woman is different. I'm not in control most of the time. Men do work quite hard to satisfy a woman because a man wants to satisfy a woman. And get off, obviously. With sex with a man, it was all about making the man want me, and want me again. There was a lot of performance and control. When I had sex with a woman for the first time, and ever since really, I don't feel I can do that performance and control. With a woman there's more of a connection, or maybe sex with a woman demands more of a connection. I mean, I've only slept with one woman but it feels like we're both more present. I find it very difficult to be present. The one time I was really present with my current partner, I cried. I had one of those orgasms that people talk about where you cry at the end. I felt like it had been too intense. It was just too much.

It was really easy to come out as a lesbian. It was just the easiest thing. I had one friend say, 'You used to *really* like sex. And you used to *really* like penises!' And I did. There was no lie there. Another friend said, 'I know what this is, you've fallen in love with one woman.' She was implying that I wasn't really gay, that I'd fallen in love with one specific woman as if *that* was the point. My parents were fine; they just wanted to know if I was still going to have kids. And wear dresses. Like I was not going to be feminine and pretty any more and it'd be such a shame! I could tell the people who had to go away and think about it for a while for their own reasons, but it didn't feel like anyone was homophobic. People take it as is and that makes me feel really good about it.

Me and my girlfriend are in a proper relationship and have been for three years and we really know each other and have a family. I love my partner and she loves me and it's a successful relationship as far as I know a successful relationship to be. Ultimately the question I have in my mind is, 'Am I actually straight but I can't cope with men and how crap they are so have gone somewhere else?' Because when I met my current partner I was at the end of my tether with men. I was pretty unhappy. I felt like I couldn't really understand men and what their needs were and why I couldn't meet them. If I picture sleeping with a man now it feels quite awkward. Funnily enough, before I got into the relationship with my partner a friend asked, 'Would you ever sleep with a woman?' I said, 'I haven't, but I would be open, if the right woman came along, to having a relationship with her.' Then it happened eight months later, which is weird.

My current girlfriend was a friend and we hung out a lot. When I first met her I felt like there was something there and I thought, 'Is it because she's gay that I'm getting feelings for her, and from her?' Every time we saw each other there was a really big chemistry and I would think about her in a sexual way – but mostly in a romantic way. I thought about the intrigue of us falling in love and then we kind of did and yeah, here we are now.

My partner has a child whom she conceived right when we got together. I knew, having been her friend for three years beforehand, that she was planning to have a child, but it was just something a friend was doing. Then she did conceive. We'd *just* slept together for the first time. We'd had a picnic and we'd talked about the future. I was happy that we'd slept together and we'd agreed that it wasn't an awful nightmare and we weren't going to run away from each other and it was all fine. Then two days later she called me and she was all kind of weird and she was like, '*Hi!*' and then she was like, 'Well, that's great, bye then.' And hung up. And I was like, 'Weird conversation.' Then she called back straight away and said, 'Actually, I called you up to tell you something and didn't know how to tell you: I'm pregnant.' I had to ask her recently what my reaction was because I couldn't remember: she said there was a long pause and I went, 'Wow.'

I think the way I looked at it was if I couldn't find a reason to leave, then there were probably a lot of reasons to stay. I could have instantly gone, 'Oh God, this is a massive commitment, what a nightmare,' but I didn't because I remember thinking, 'Imagine myself without this relationship; do I feel better? No, not really, I don't feel better. I really like her and maybe even love her already.' There was no reason to make a big drama out of it. I didn't know what it was going to mean, I didn't know much about babies. It was just a day at a time.

So she had a child, Edward, who lives with us half the week and half the week with his father who is a good friend of hers who lives round the corner and they co-parent together. There was no sexual exchange between them; it was completely, you know, a transaction, like a sperm donor. He's gay and lives with his partner. And Edward is the child of all of us. He's my partner's and his father's son but I co-parent in that Edward lives in the house with us and we do things together and I act as a parent in as much as doing the daily routine and cooking dinner and all that sort of thing. I don't get up in the night! And it's just him; there are no other children.

I was thinking today when Edward was screaming his head off that I can't have my own children, I'm too controlling and I don't have that patience a parent needs. I can handle Edward because he's only there half the week. There's this glorious thing where we all have a break. Could I do this all the time? I don't think that I can. It would just be hell for any child I had. And I would be beating myself up the entire time until I worked a lot of that stuff out. I feel like I'm destined to help children in some other way. But direct parenting isn't for me.

I was trained to be a good girl. My mum is an academic and an active alcoholic. She was very shut down, and me and my sister and brother got very shut down around her. There was a lot of avoiding drama, and people-pleasing, and trying to be a good girl. My dad is a lecturer and he left when I was twelve and my dad leaving was my first heartbreak. I didn't process that grief, and without a doubt my compulsive romanticising and the controlling of sexual relationships was the result of that heartbreak. Otherwise everything else was pretty normal, everybody acting out in their own way, but nothing major. I went to university and did languages and then I went to live in Spain. I had quite an intense relationship for a year with a Moroccan guy, lots of drama and screaming and great sex – exhausting!

I think about sex a lot. All the time, and I always have. The first time I had sex I remember thinking, '*My God*, this is *just* the best thing *ever*. I can't believe I waited this long.' And I had a lot of it; it was really fun. I had a relationship with porn a lot during my teens and my twenties; it wasn't daily but whenever I wanted it. There were periods when it was rather a lot! I transferred that to compulsive sexual relationships so there was less emphasis on watching porn and more on doing. I was in a cycle of compulsive sex and trying to find something in people I was never going to find.

Porn can be really triggering – *instantly* triggering. It has *never* failed to turn me on *ever*. It is so quick; it is almost instant. It is like I am illuminated by it. I don't need to watch it for longer than two minutes. There is that feeling of how quick it is, and how powerful, *really* powerful and really fast. Sex in relationships is not really powerful and not really fast. Not for me, yet, anyway. Afterwards I have no desire to keep watching. As soon as I've had an orgasm it is like I am watching white fuzz, it is like, 'What's that? Turn it off.' That's the point of porn, you just get off and that's it.

I've *always* thought that the most successful sexual relationship I've had was between myself and porn because I'm in total control. I can choose what I want to watch, I can choose what I want to do, and that's perfect for me. I'm talking about porn where men and women are having sex, not hardcore porn or things featuring animals and all the rest of it. Because I've always watched male porn I was wondering if even though I'm in a gay relationship I'm not actually gay. I don't know if I'm bisexual or whether I'm gay or whether it matters.

I've used the fantasy/masturbation ritual since I was twelve when I started masturbating. I saw pornography really early, about eleven, and then I had a fantasy made for me that I could use. The man in command works for me, particularly the feeling of the woman being overpowered, not really aggressively or violently. I know that's not healthy. Throwing against the wall quite roughly always comes into my fantasies. If I fantasise about a woman it's me pushing her against a wall. If I fantasise about a man it's a man pushing me against a wall or a door. It's passionate. It's about letting go of inhibitions and doing whatever I want to do, losing control, and for the other person to be okay with that. I've got this weird fantasy that keeps coming into my mind about being on the TV programme *Question Time* – so ridiculous! I'm asked my opinion and I have the answers to a social conundrum. I would have the best answer and that would make the person fall in love with me. There's something about it being intellectual. It's that thing of, I'll be really loved for the things I say as well as the things I do.

A large part of my day can be spent in fantasies, not really achieving anything. There's a lot of time-wasting. I can use fantasies to zone out of my life in the same way I can zone out with anything else, like sugar or alcohol. I'm talking about compulsive fantasy; something that drops into my mind, like my brain's wired that way. I'm now realising the fantasising is addictive in nature. At first, masturbation was something I would do when I felt lonely, and then it became a way to deal with a lot of things like feeling anxious, feeling out of sorts. There's something about making a decision: it's helpful to masturbate. To go into fantasy and then masturbate helps me forget about what I'm supposed to be doing. Going into fantasyland when I feel tired is completely automatic and it does feel addictive, and therefore I cannot stop doing it. I cannot stop fantasising without help and without working through some issues. Fantasy comes, knocks into my mind and then it's there. I can either play it out or I can do what I do now, which is to try and reject it from my mind and think up something else. I don't watch porn now. I don't know if I'll go back to watching it. It feels like I've put that down.

I find it very difficult to be present with someone all the way through sex because I don't think I've ever done that. Man or woman, it's the same thing, I'm basically fantasising. Fantasising helps me to feel that I'm *not* in the relationship, that I'm actually somewhere else doing something else, and that's a huge comfort. If I take that away, do I actually like sex? And if I do like sex, how do I like sex, and who with? I'd like to know that. I'd like to know if some of the feelings I had with men were real or whether it was all approval-seeking. The fantasy comes in to help me; otherwise I can't do sex. If I don't fantasise I get really anxious and I feel like I can't cope with being in the relationship and I want to leave and run away. But now I don't want to use fantasy to control my life because my past relationships have been damaged by it.

I've talked to my partner about compulsive fantasising and I'm not sure that she understands what I mean. She definitely is aware of my aggressive response to having her reach out to me when I'm fantasising. I get very aggressive and defensive. It would be better if I wasn't in the fantasies, then there wouldn't be this area of my being that she can't get to and if she does, it's met with an angry shutdown. It's a private place I go to quite aggressively. It is always me on my own. Fantasising feels like isolation now. The more I try to engage with other people in romantic relationships and in friendship the more I realise I need other people.'

# 3

# Shop assistant

Sigourney, 38, Watford

*'I've never ever, ever had sex like that before'*

'I work as a trainee manager in a large fashion chain. I'm just a trainee manager, so it's not like an actual manager. It's really, really hard work. I'd say I'm a hard worker. People come in and buy a lot of clothes. It's pay day this week so they're cashy. They're so cashy. Some of the bankers can be snobs. They're really untidy. They drag up the clothes and they treat us who work there with no respect. Obviously, whatever they mess, we have to tidy up. They leave a drink, we have to pick it up. Had women come and vomit on the floor. Women being on their period and leaving pads on the floor of the changing rooms. We've had someone poo on the floor. It's gross! You'd be surprised. There was one time where the customers actually had a fight and a security guard had to stop it, just over being in the queue. I'm a big girl and I see women who are big put on a size 14 and I can see it's not going on. I've had to cut a woman out of a dress because she couldn't get out of it. I could have told her it was too tight. It was funny, I was like, 'What made you put that on ...?'

I like to look nice and I like when women make the effort to look nice. Recently they told me I've got to wear sophisticated clothes because I'm in the Ladies Modern Classics department so they want me to dress more lady-type, no jeans and crop tops – which is my favourite! I don't mind; it's a challenge to get up every morning and put tights on, which I haven't done since school. When I wear tighter clothes, it emphasises me and then it's like, 'Oh, here we go.' Well, I've got big boobs. And obviously the guys that come in are not going to be like looking at my face, they're going to be looking at my chest.

You do get perverts. A lot of men buy women's skinny jeans because the cut's different. One guy put a pair on but they were *too* tight around his crotch and he came out of the changing room: 'So... how do you think these are?' And I could see the outline of it – his willy – and I was like, 'Yeah, you need a bigger size.' He was like, 'Do you reckon?' I was like, '*Yeah!* You do.' And I just couldn't look at his face, I was like, I can see your tool. I went red and my manager comes, and I was like, 'I can't deal with it, can you go in there and take over, please?' It was embarrassing. Some men are proud of what they've got and they want to be like, 'I've got this, I've got that.' But I don't come to work for this! Men will come up to me and say, 'Excuse me, I don't know what my size is in boxer shorts, can you tell what size I am?' and they'll just stand there and expect me to look down. And I'm like 'Small?' And they say, 'I'm not Small, no no no. You mean Extra Large?' and I'm like, 'Well, you asked.' Some of them you can have fun with, you can have a giggle.

I was with my first two kids' dad for seven years. When I was nineteen, I was going to Battersea and I ended up in Tooting Broadway, and I said, 'I've got lost,' and I asked him for directions! Yeah! And he start talking to me and we start talking and then we's a couple. He's Jamaican. I'm half-Jamaican. The relationship broke because he's seven years older than me and he's acting fourteen years younger than me. He's got this lazy attitude, he used to just smoke weed and we never used to have any money and when you've got two kids and you're both working and you still can't make ends meet, what's the point of being with someone? He was working, but all our money was spent on weed. I was smoking myself and when I got to twenty-four, I was like: this is not life. I stopped smoking and I could feel myself pulling myself right off him: 'I don't want to be with you no more because I don't want this.'

I just wasn't happy. Every day I was getting up and I was going through the motions. Sex side was down and he didn't really notice it and I was thinking, most of his friends were players and they slept around, so he was probably getting it elsewhere which is why he was okay with it. A player is someone who sleeps with other women. Just dates casually. He always says no he wasn't a player, but I don't believe it because *all* of his friends have multiple girlfriends. I wouldn't say that's a Jamaican thing; I'd say it's a black thing. They find it hard to just be with one person. My son's godfather, one time he had three girlfriends and I knew the three of them. A lot of girls in the West Indian community would accept it. The three women know he has children with all of them because he would have his children all together. I'm just like, 'Oh no.' That mentality is completely different to me, because he's from south London. Because I've always lived in Watford, my mum didn't really go around with a lot of black people.

I couldn't bear him to even touch me, I was over the

relationship and obviously I felt bad; my sons, they loved their dad, and they want to be with their dad but I couldn't do it. I didn't leave until I was twenty-six. But I had my mum and she was supporting me.

He still smokes now. He don't give me no money for his kids. He sees them. He's a good dad. There's no money, but if they need any support, homework, whatever, he's there 100 per cent for them. He doesn't work. He is ill now, he's got Crohn's disease. He's got one other child since. Like, he's really young, really immature. He's all right, he's just happy being a young older guy! Which I didn't want.

So I was with the first two's dad for seven years and we had two kids then we broke up and six months later I met the twins' dad. I met him through my mum's husband. He's African. I was in my African stage. I quite like African men! I like the accent; oh my God, I like the accent. Sexually, they know exactly what to say to a woman. They just know. They just make you feel – I reckon – really nice. Their mouth is sweet. Like, 'Hey, beautiful! You look really pretty today.' I can be really angry and they say something and I think to myself, 'You idiot', and I end up smiling and it's nice. I like the accent. Yeah. I fancied him.

When I met him sometimes I would bleed continuously for weeks with my period. I was having all these blood tests and they couldn't find out what was wrong with me. And I thought, I'm not going to be able to have any more children again. I'd got two, which was fine, and then I met him and we must have had sex and then I got pregnant! One of the few times we had sex I got pregnant with the twins. It was two months into the relationship and I was like, 'Oh my God, oh God, what am I going to do? I'm going to have an abortion.' And he was, 'No, keep it, we're going to have it.' When I was six weeks I was having cramps because of my problems. We went to the hospital and they gave me a scan and she was like, 'Oops, there's one baby and there's the other one,' and I was like, 'Oh my God!'

He has always owned his own business, a plumber; very career-minded. I think some black people watch what everyone else is doing and believe that they should have everything – or more than the other person – and I wasn't brought up that way. He wanted his own home. I live on a council estate. He didn't want to live on a council estate no more; he wanted us to live in a house. He wanted us to live in Exeter, which is a very expensive place to live in. I know nobody there. In Watford I've got friends, if I need anyone to pick up the twins I've got that. If I move to Exeter it's for me to start all over again. I'm not going to say it couldn't have happened, but it would have been a gradual thing. I'd have to leave my work, get a new job. He went to Exeter. I don't know if he's single now – I'm not interested in what he's doing.

I was with him for ten years. We broke up. It was the worst time of my life. Cos I think for me he was *the* one. I could have done anything for him, anything he wanted, cut my right hand off, and given it to him. Yep, broke my heart. It was bad. The bigger twin, he's still got this anger, he says that his dad doesn't love him. 'My daddy doesn't love me.' He's dramatic. He still sees his dad.

When we were together my partner used to always put me down, say I'm fat, I shouldn't wear black clothes, why have I got to wear false hair in my hair? And I started to go within myself and dress not like me. He didn't like a low-cut top. I'd be showing my assets – I've got big boobs, I've got a big bum. I reckon that as a black woman, that's what we do – we show our assets, what makes us, defines us. He was trying to take that away from me and it was draining. So, since being single I'm wearing what makes me happy.

My other boyfriends were black. Serious sexual relationships always been with black. Since I've broken up with the twins' dad I've slept with two white guys. They're different. Yes. Oh my God, in sex style, yes. A lot of black guys have this thing, 'Black men, they don't go down.' Some do oral sex but I've never been with one, whereas white guys say it's their speciality; they go down without any question. With black guys, everything that you do is a secret. If he goes down on you, you wouldn't tell nobody. If you do anal, you wouldn't tell nobody. It's a secret. And black men have the biggest willies ever. Which they don't! They're not small but they're not the biggest. There's no difference. I'm just speaking by my own experiences so I can't really judge about anybody else.

My ex – the twins' dad – was like, 'Who comes first wins,' and obviously he used to come first. So! And then I wouldn't come. After twenty minutes? And there's no oral? I wouldn't come. So it's a bit boring. It was about thrusting as hard as possible. There was no 'We're going to make love; we're going to enjoy it for what it is. We're going to stop, we're going to kiss, we're going to caress, we're going to touch, we're going to know each other.' It's an intimate act. It doesn't become intimate when someone's just ramming you. It isn't enjoyable for me. So when we broke up it was a relief because we had sex right up until he left. I told myself it was normal. When you love somebody then you kind of accept it, like if your man's got a small penis, you accept it. So that's what I done with myself.

I never used to feel sexually fulfilled. Until my first time with the Mexican guy recently. He works in a hotel. He's twenty-eight. We'd been speaking for months, I went on the first date, then went on the second date, I thought, maybe he's not into me, I'm just going to go on this date, maybe we could be good friends because the conversation is fun. And then one thing led to another and I was like '... *Fuck me*: this is actually good'. I've never ever, ever had sex like that before. And it kind of shocked me. I didn't think that a white guy could make me feel sexually fulfilled. He couldn't come, so it was long, like three hours. An hour and a half, then a break, then another hour and a half. It was like I was going to die of exhaustion. Like, this has never happened to me before!

Like with orgasm, before if I came it was almost like I was embarrassed, like I'd keep it to myself. I wouldn't say, 'I'm coming.' We was going and I thought, 'Okay, I've already come, la-la-la-la-la,' and then he came and I could feel it, and I was like, 'Oh my God!' Never in my life has that happened. And then the second time we had it he could just feel my body twitching and I was like, '*I've never come like that before!*' It was a shock. I don't know if it was because it was so long that I hadn't had sex for. We used condoms so it's not like it was unprotected sex. There was no alcohol involved, I had a clear head. It was the weirdest thing ever. I had to meet my friend afterwards and I was like, 'This has happened! It has never happened before!' She was like, 'You just got some good sex!' I was like, 'Where's he been all my life?' And it's not like his willy was *massive*, I'd put it at seven inches, which is quite big; average size. So it was good. I've had orgasms from penetration before. Yeah, I have, but not like that. It blowed my mind. That's what it's done. And even he was like, 'Uh!'

When I left, I went to McDonald's and I quickly had some food. I was like, 'God, I have to get up tomorrow.' The next morning I was like, 'I'm sore!' I had bruises – I don't know if I've got them still – but I had loads on my arm from where he was gripping my arm. I was all over the place. He was massaging me, he was rubbing my neck. The sex was different, I've never had a massage and sex together, from behind.

I went to a friend, 'I don't know where this is going, but it's doing my head in if I can't have him in my life. I need this guy in my life, like permanently, that's how it is now. I don't ever chase guys and it's killing me that he still hasn't contacted me.' Some of my friends are like, 'Call him,' I'm like, 'Not doing it.' Even if I can have one more night with him I'll be happy!

I never used to have sexual fantasies until one of my work colleagues put it into my head about a threesome. She said, 'It's the most best feeling ever as you as the woman are in control.' Just having two guys all over me. Yeah. That's what I said to the Mexican guy. He said, 'Why two men?' I couldn't have another woman there because I could be vying for attention and I can't see myself kissing a woman like that. It would have to be two men. Unless the two men were into each other!

If you watch a porno you see the woman doing everything; I think, 'Oh, I'd love that confidence.' I don't have that. I don't have a great sexual history. I've not slept with a lot of guys. Probably under ten, so sexually I don't know stuff, and I feel shy in bed, I don't really have the confidence. I'm not really into anal at all. I have tried it, it's very uncomfortable. I suppose it's something you *could* get used to if you were having it frequently. Some things I think to myself, 'Just do it!' And other stuff I think, 'No, don't do it! No!' My dad used to beat my mum up so I don't feel like being tied up would be my thing and I'm not a fan of spanking. I'm not really into pain. I've done everything I want to do.

I love being a woman. Oh my God, I love my boobs, I love that they're big. I like them, even though some men can be cheesy, like, 'Can I touch? Can I put my face in?' Yeah! On a Friday night in town: '*Please*! Can I touch?' I say, 'You've had too much to drink, go away.' I just find it funny. I'm like, 'I see you've got a ring on your finger, go to your wife and ask your wife. Do that to your wife.' I like my legs – they're long. I like their shape. I like my bum, obviously. I've got a bum that sticks out; it's quite shapely. And men like it. Every man likes it: white, black, Asian. Managers. Girls at work touch it, slap it, pinch it! If I'm walking in they're like, 'Sigourney!' *Pinch*. They pinch it. I'm like, 'Oh my God!' It's nice.

I *love* the fact my body's changed after having four children. My belly, my stretch marks – I love them. My children, they made my body what it is, from a young woman to what it is now. I look at my kids, I think, 'They done this to my body, but look at them, they're mine, I made them.' Then my breasts. I breastfed them, that's my intimate bond between me and my children. Yeah, so I like being a woman, I wouldn't change it, apart from childbirth! But everyone would probably say that. I just enjoy being a girl.

I've got the best of worlds being British and being black. Being black as a woman is fun. I'm light; a lot of people don't really consider me black because I am mixed. My mum's Trinidadian, my dad's from St Kitts but they're mixed-race on my dad's side. A lot of other black women think, 'You light-skinned people make me sick,' and that we think we're better than people who are darker than us. But I would love to be really, really black – to be darker. I find it mysterious, sexy. I like darker women.

I reckon I'm the kind of person no matter what colour I was, I'd embrace everything about being a woman. We've just got it over men sexually. We can dress a certain way. Like today, if I pull my top low I'm sexy. I've got the hat on, I've got lip gloss in my car, my eyes are done. Then I can take my hat off, pull my hair out, curl it up, put jeans on, heels on, some make-up on and I'm somebody else. Every day I could be a different person. My friend always asks me, 'What's the look today?'

# 4

# Transgender

Margery, 71, London

*'I went through puberty at fifty-seven'*

'When I was twenty-one I met my other half. Met at a dance in Hackney Downs. A day of infamy! Day of destiny. That was September '65 and by August '67 we were married. Five kids in twelve years. You may wonder how. So do I. When I was a man I wanted to be a woman so I found it almost impossible to perform. I wanted to have sex as a woman. I'd rather be underneath than on top. I don't think she really understood that at all. Wives don't normally understand; I wouldn't expect them to. I wouldn't expect any wife understanding their husband wanting to take the woman's role; the subservient role. Most wives wouldn't understand that; well, normal wives wouldn't. Some wives like domination.

At five I wanted to be a girl. I saw my mother's bra in a cupboard and something in me snapped. I can still see it: salmon pink, shiny. And I had to have it. From then on I was obsessed with women's underwear. Fetishistic fantasies, that's what the psychiatrist called it. I had a fetish about women's underwear. I just wanted it. To touch it, hold it, wear it. All day. My fantasies were about masturbation wearing women's knickers. That turned me on. That really turned me on. But that's not unusual. A lot of men like wearing women's knickers. Yeah, I reckon so. Not that it's generally talked about but I think it's true.

And I had a thing about women's clothes, not just underwear, but nice dresses, two-piece suits, everything. My mother caught me with her dress on when I was twelve. She got a surprise. So did I because I didn't think she was coming home early for lunch. She said, 'Oh, take it off!' That same outfit I've seen in the Victoria & Albert Museum, it's a John Frieda outfit, 1954. Very smart. Sex was very taboo when I was a child. No one ever mentioned sex – it's a wonder they had sex actually.

I wanted to be a woman when I was getting married. But I thought it would go away. I thought it would just wear off and I'd be normal like everyone else. I was completely wrong. It got more intense. I couldn't get rid of this thing out of my head. Whatever I was doing it was in my head. I was washing-up, I was thinking about becoming a woman. When I was in the bath, I was thinking about it. I was eating dinner, I was thinking about it. I was at work, I was thinking about it. It was what was in my head all the time.

I didn't know if having sex would solve it because I'd never had sex before. We were both virgins when we got married. I had sex when I was married. Many times. Didn't enjoy it, though, it was a chore. Because she wanted it. I never wanted it. I wanted to be penetrated but I didn't have a vagina. My body felt all wrong. I hated the old penis. I hated it. I hated the sight of it, the look of it, the feel of it. Just hated it. Because it's unnatural. What woman would want to have a penis? I wanted to have sex as a woman. Yeah. But I didn't have a vagina. Very frustrating. Like someone in a wheelchair who wants to walk but their body won't let them. And I wanted to have the child. I've always been jealous of pregnant women. So I did the next best thing. Don't know why, to be honest, I had so many kids!

They say 'trapped in the wrong body'. That's a very true way of putting it. I was never gay. I had a day or two thinking I'll try and be camp, and it just wasn't me. I'm not at all camp. I'm common! You'd never see me acting in a camp way. Women don't! What woman acts in a camp way? No one. Gay men do. No woman would act like that, it would look ridiculous.

I didn't tell the wife how I felt. I didn't dare. I never told anyone until 1991 when I was forty-seven. That's not unusual; a lot of people keep it very hidden. When I did tell people, no one believed me. That was the funny thing. I told Mrs R I wanted to be a woman and she thought I was having a joke. Mrs R, the wife. Mrs R, I call her. Everyone thought I was having a laugh, having a joke. A weird joke. I was being serious; they thought I was having a laugh. Can't make it up, can you?

I tried to talk to Mrs R but she just blew up and I thought, I'm not talking to her. This is impossible. I couldn't talk to her about changing sex; anything else you were okay. And to be honest, up to a point I didn't understand it. When I was a teenager I would go to Foyle's bookshop but there were only books written in 1901 by Freud, and Krafft-Ebing in Germany talking about conversions. No idea what they were talking about. I suppose you could say that I was suffering. I wouldn't choose to be transgender, I must admit. It's a cross you bear. I think in life things happen and you get tested as a human being.

The first twenty years weren't too bad with Mrs R. The last fifteen were hell. Well, she got very menopausal, financial pressures, kids; this feeling I had got stronger, and we came out of sync. So we just sort of grew apart, I think. We had a lot of rows about how I felt, and I decided at that point I couldn't, wouldn't, talk about it. I clamped up and I told myself if the opportunity to express my feminine side came up again I'd take it. And in 1997, six years later, Mrs R became very absentminded. I didn't notice it at first. Eventually she was diagnosed with Alzheimer's, you see. At fifty-three. And it got progressively worse. By 2001, I was her full-time carer. She was doubly incontinent. Very tiring being a carer, because I couldn't get out of the house. Worked from home, couldn't really go into the office.

Then, 8th January 2002, she suddenly decided she wouldn't eat dinner. She said, 'I've already eaten dinner.' I said, 'No, you haven't' – because I was doing the cooking. We had a hospital appointment booked and they kept her in. And I thought, I've got a day off. Two days later, 10th January, I decided, 'This is it, I'm doing it – because I can't see her coming back.' And I decided, 'This is it, this is the day of decision.' I started buying women's clothes, underwear, make-up, anything. I rang up the doctor's office and saw him 11th March 2002. Things began to move now. He said to me, 'I suppose you want hormones?' I said, 'Yes please!' He wrote a prescription. Went round the chemist, got them within half an hour.

Female hormones make you weak. I have lost a lot of muscle power, but I think at seventy-one you do. What the doctor said to me at the beginning was I would grow breasts like my mother but two sizes smaller, I'd be very tempera-mental because I would be on hormones, and I'd probably gain a lot of weight. Well, I'm not at all temperamental. And the breasts are much fuller – the hormones made them grow. Fabulous, fabulous! Love it. They grew very slowly; after about two years I hardly saw anything.

I had started to visit trans clubs, started to make friends who told me about a private clinic. Around that time I had a really mad period, that Christmas I did twelve parties in thirteen days: trans clubs, discos and dancing. I was exhausted afterwards, I thought, it's bloody hard work being a woman! Constant partying; one pub after another.

I was dressing as a man and a woman. I was getting up and dressing as a woman in the morning. After lunch, I was dressing as a man to go to work, then being a woman again in the evening. You can't do that for very long. It screws your head up. I wanted to dress as a woman. I went through the stages of being a transvestite first. There's an enormous difference between someone who's a transsexual and someone who's a transvestite, it's not the same at all. A transvestite doesn't want to get rid of his bits. Whereas a transsexual wants to go the whole way. Everything.

There's a thing called the Harry Benjamin Gender Dysmorphia Scale. Harry Benjamin was a noted psychiatrist in the 1960s in New York. Gender dysmorphia is a big word meaning mental confusion. Harry Benjamin realised people with gender dysmorphia actually form a pattern, and he classified them from stage one to stage six. Makes sense. I've painted a picture of it; it's called Gender Disorientation Scowl. Stage one is a guy who dresses as a woman once a month and gets a kick out of it. Stage two is when someone might dress once a week. Stage three is someone who dresses every day. Stage four is a non-surgical transsexual: you live as a man as a woman. Stage five is what they call a true transsexual, moderate intensity: everything but the operation. It's not essential. Stage six is you do the whole lot, everything, got to have the operation. There's no question, you've just got to do it. And that was me: stage six.

August 2002, I'd made a lot of friends at trans clubs and we went to Brighton Pride. I decided to take no male clothes at all. It was Friday, Saturday, Sunday, and it was brilliant. No problem whatsoever. Then in October I heard about this place in Somerset. It's like a holiday camp for trannies. There were about a hundred and twenty people on the site. I dressed as a woman for eleven days, non-stop. Brilliant. I came back to London and I went to the office and the boss said to me, 'Oh, you don't look very well.' And I said, 'Don't I?' He said, 'Have you got a personal problem?' because he knew about Mrs R, and I said, 'Actually' – I thought, buggered if I'm not just going to tell him, I don't care, I'm just going to tell him – I said, 'I'm changing sex.' I mean, there's no way of getting round it, you can't say it in a roundabout way, can you? And he said – this is really like *Monty Python* – he said, 'Well, I'll have to speak to someone in Human Resources about this.'

He said to me, 'Human Resources looked into it and they couldn't find anyone.' I'm working for a building company, there was seventeen thousand people in the company and they couldn't find anyone else like me. There was, but they didn't know, obviously. Then my boss said, 'If you want to come as a woman, you better let us know.' 'Well,' I said, 'I'm coming on Monday morning!' Turned up Monday morning. Wig. Dress. Everyone stared for about two minutes. Two-minute wonder. I'd been working there six years. There were a hundred and seventy people in the office. I reckon I could have pulled half of them men!

I thought it was brilliant because it was moving fast now. Two months later, my friend changed her name to Pam. I thought, I'm doing that. So I saw a solicitor – fifty quid it cost – and legally changed my name by deed poll. Margery, because it's clear, it's unambiguous and it's old-fashioned and you can't be muddled by it. It's definitely a woman's name. And my second name is Dawn because my middle name was Derek, so I kept the same initials; it's easier for signing cheques. I'm practical! New dawn, new life. Easy. When I changed my name the person I was died that day. It was quite an emotional day. I was fifty-seven at that time. It was like someone died, but another person was born.

By June 2003, I was having laser treatment – it's painful. They put this thing on your face and it kills the hairs. Six sessions. I've never had any hair on my chest. Or I've shaved it off. Had some on the arms. July 2003, I went back to the private clinic. I said to the doctor, 'I'm thinking about surgery now.' He said to me, 'You're ready, are you?' And I said, 'Yeah, I think so.' Because I'm a person who can't do half a job. Being me, I took some very far-reaching decisions very quickly. I took an extreme position. There was no question, there was no 'Do I do this or do I do that?' No, you have surgery, you dress as a woman, you change your name, everything, everything, everything. Whatever needs to be done you do. Some people think, 'Oh, I don't know, shall I change my name? It's a big step. Got to tell people, got to tell family.' I said, 'Whatever it is I've got to do, sod it, what the hell.' Bit scary but ...

So the GP arranged for me to see a private surgeon, a Mr Evans, in a very nice hospital. Cost me nine and a half thousand quid. I paid for it! I want things now; I don't want to wait. It's a very slow process to go through the National Health Service; a lot of people take five years. There's a big hospital in London that treats two and a half thousand people a year. They do three operations a week. The hospital really will not entertain you going on hormones and having surgery until you show total commitment. You have to do what's called a real-life test: you've got to live as a woman for two years. If you're half-hearted – 'Oh, I don't know, I don't know' – you ain't going to get surgery. But I'm a different person from what I used to be. I used to be a person who planned and waited patiently for things. Now I'm not. I want it now. Mr Evans booked the surgery, and it was booked for 7th March 2004. Two years after Mrs R went into hospital. So I actually lived as a woman for seventeen months before I had surgery.

Then I had to see a psychiatrist at Hove to get a confirmation for the surgery. Some people actually regret it. One in ten is called a regretter. I said to him, 'Well, I know what I'm doing. I'm fifty-eight, if I make a mistake, it's down to me.' If you're fourteen years old you might not know what you're doing, but at fifty-eight if you don't know what you're doing, you never will. By that point I'd been married, I'd had five kids, I'd worked for forty years as a chartered surveyor, I owned a house, if I can't be in control of my life by then, I never will. So the psychiatrist just said, 'Right' and he rubber-stamped it and that was it. And so at that point there was a hundred and forty-four days to go. To the surgery.

Eventually March 2004 came round. The operation was booked for Tuesday. Monday morning I go down the hospital in Brighton with me suitcase, booked in. By the evening I'm terrified, because I've got surgery the next day. Some people, they think you can put your coat on and walk out. But I thought, 'If I do that, I'll be back in two years, there's no choice. I've got to see it through.'

Tuesday came round. Remember waking up after surgery and thinking '*Six times seven equals forty-two – I can think.*' Because people had told me stories of how they'd seen demons afterwards. The operation was bloody painful! You've got to be mad to do it. On the first night I was on a liquid diet in hospital. I had this bandage right up, very tight, and so what happened over a day or two I began to fill up with wind so the wind is pushing up, the bandages are pushing down and after three days it's fucking agony. I'm beginning to think, 'What have I done?' I couldn't wee because I was so swollen. I had a catheter stuck to me leg. After five days the bandages came off and I had a bath; they helped me. I actually got up and collapsed. I had to have an oxygen mask. That's normal, you know, most people do. The fifth day, they took the bandages out.

Inside there's a big hole where the vagina is. The penis is inside out. They used the skin. It's a normal vagina. A man couldn't tell the difference. A man wouldn't know unless I told him. I'm told a lesbian could, but not a normal guy. He might find it more difficult physically, because I wouldn't open as much as an actual woman, I don't think. Having been married as a man I know about these things. It smells different. A natural-born woman has certain odours from her vagina which someone who's trans doesn't have. The depth is limited as a trans woman, there's just a wall, whereas a woman who has babies has got a whole thing behind it: cervix, uterus, and all the rest of it. I wee like a woman. Sitting down. It's great! I love it! It's one of the pleasures of being a woman, having a wee. It feels natural. I've got a clitoris. Oh, it works! Oh yes! Oh yes! When I had the surgery my body stopped producing testosterone so there was nothing to stop my breasts growing. When I had surgery they began to grow very much better. I went through puberty at fifty-seven. What a girl of twelve would be, I was that.

I left hospital on day eight and went to a B&B in Brighton

and I stayed there for eight weeks – I thought, 'If I'm ever going to spend money on me, this is it.' Every day I wandered round Brighton looking in shop windows. I reasoned, 'If I walk around the streets all day I'm going to heal up faster.' I went through stabbing pains as nerve endings reformed. You've got to be tough to do this, I tell you! You've got to be really tough to have a sex change and have surgery. Physically and mentally tough. I wouldn't recommend it for light-hearted people. A lot of my friends say, 'Oh, I can do it.' No you can't, you've got to be tough.

The children – bloody hell – they were quite shocked, but they just have to put up with it. The youngest is thirty-five. I mean, I don't have children, they're adults. They call me Dad, their husbands and wives call me Margery, and the grandchildren call me Nana. I think it's gradually dawning on the oldest grandchildren. Mrs R, she died. She turned into a vegetable. She didn't know anything, not at all. My oldest son is freaked out about it. The rest are okay. He's inherited my worst male attributes: he likes arguing with people, very argumentative, hates gay people, I think. He assumes I'm gay and I'm not. I tell him to sod off. Well, it's just too late, they'll have to lump it, won't they? I'm not reverting back to being a bloke. Why should I? I live my life for me, not for other people. I'm in charge; I give the orders now, if you see what I mean.

When I meet people today they think I'm a woman. Well, I am. They don't know and, unless I speak in a really deep voice, they won't know. My voice has probably changed very slightly. If I went round in big wigs and high heels people would stare at me, but I don't. I haven't worn make-up for thirteen years. Can't be bothered. I'm not trying to pull. People treat me differently now. I would say they're nicer, on the whole. Men are much more accommodating to me as a woman, they call me 'love'. Blinking cheek! I like it. Makes me laugh. I always get a seat on the train. I'm like an old dear with my shopping basket. I have this strange feeling I'm turning into Miss Marple, with my little hat and my flat shoes, a bit nosey and bossy. I'm a sensible conservative. I used to be a man but I'm very conventional. I just want to be absolutely normal. I'm in a conventional neighbourhood, living a conventional life, doing conventional things. I'm totally normal, more or less. And it's easy. For me it's very, very easy to be normal. There's no effort. Everyone tells me I'm cool and trendy and I think I'm quite boring actually! I'm just so conventional.

I've been both a man and a woman. It's odd, that. I can't say there's many have done that. Not many people have had an orgasm as a man and as a woman, I'll tell you. A woman's is better. As a man you just want to relieve your tension. A man's orgasm is short and sharp and quick. A woman's is much deeper and longer-lasting, I would say. It's much more pleasurable to masturbate as a woman – I've got a vibrator – than it was to masturbate as a man. It goes over a longer time, it's much more intense. It blows your mind completely. With women it's definitely much more with the whole body rather than just the head and the hands of the man when men masturbate.

I was very straight as a man. Heterosexual. Now as a woman I sometimes fancy guys. When I was a man I never fancied men at all. Now, occasionally I might see a man and think, 'Oh, very nice! Bit young for me, but very nice.' I'm basically bisexual, you see. I wasn't so much before. Sexuality is fluid. Very fluid. I can be much more feminine one day than another, or much more masculine. Because I'm really quite blokey as a woman. I trained as a quantity surveyor and I worked on building sites till the end of 2003. That's why I'm doing the building works on my house. My qualification with my old name is on the wall. I'm actually an Associate Member of the Chartered Institute of Builders. It's odd, but it's me.

I'm still a virgin as a woman. Told my kids I'm a virgin! Because I haven't found a man to fall in love with. It might happen; I fancy men sometimes but they've got to be quite good-looking, sober, clean and intelligent. 'It's asking a lot,' as someone said to me. Who knows? It might happen. I can't think it will, but it might. I do feel curious to try sex with a man. Oh yes. But I'm waiting for the right man, that's the thing. There are clearly Mr Wrongs but very few Mr Rights, you see. I'm not bothered. I've had my days of being married: thirty-four years. You get nine years for murder!

I have sexual fantasies. Oh yes. Of having sex with men. Yeah, yeah, yeah, yeah. Quite conventional fantasies. Having normal sex face to face. Not up the backside, you know! I don't really think about it a lot, to be honest. I think as you get older your sex life wanes a bit. I don't know though: my mother-in-law got married at eighty-seven to her second husband. Shocked the kids, I can tell you!

As a woman, I'm much more controlling. I'm much more dominant, much more bossy than I was as a man. As a man I was very introvert, if there was an office party I'd always be at the back, not getting involved. I never got drunk at the front, laughing. I'm a totally different person as a woman. My entire personality's been released. My energy levels have gone through the roof. I've become a lot more confident. Miles happier. Now I get up in the morning and I think, What am I going to do today? I want to do things today. I became a workaholic when I became a woman. What I really noticed is that I can't sit still and do nothing. I've got to be doing things all the time. As a man I'd sit and do nothing. Now I'm multi-tasking.

I've got to be painting pictures, got to go out, got to be out in the West End talking to people, talking to gallery owners and having fun and going to museums and art galleries. I talk to friends and we say, 'What would have happened if we'd never done this?' I'd be the same age but a lot older. If I hadn't changed I'd be incredibly depressed as a bloke. I know that. I would be sitting at home with no friends, no social life, not wanting to do anything, contacting the kids every now and then. I wouldn't have painted a picture. Now, I go partying. My entire creative energy has been released. Sexual energy, I suppose, has been released.

You would think on the surface it would be easier to be born trans now. I'm not so sure. I think attitudes haven't really changed that much, as much as people would make you believe on Channel 4. Been to lots of meetings with transgender people and they talk about their lives. Being trans is becoming more prevalent. It's in the water, I think. Actually, perhaps that's not as far-fetched as it sounds. There's a lot of oestrogen in the tap water these days. And it's to do with the brain. There's a little bit in the hypothalamus, it's twice as large in the male brain. I think people are born with a female brain or a male brain; it controls your gender identity. I was born with a female brain. Definitely.

How it seems to me now – which I didn't really understand at the time – is, I was never male. Everyone assumed I was. But I was always a woman. When I had surgery I reverted to what I should have been. I got rid of a birth defect. Everything became right. The lights all went on: bang! Everything went from black and white into colour. Everything became normal. The funny thing was, years ago I thought if I ever did this it would be incredibly difficult and it would be awkward as a family and people would laugh at me. I thought it would be totally impossible. When it came to it, it was the easiest thing I've ever done. It was incredibly easy, but then I was never a man. It's been the main experience in my life. Nothing comes close to it in seventy-one years. The best thing I've ever done. The most satisfying thing I've ever done. Definitely. Without a doubt.

It's been fabulous, my experience of this. Fabulous being a woman. Fabulous. I was saying to my friend the other day, 'I'd do it again tomorrow. The operation and everything. No questions.' It's now been thirteen years. It feels completely natural now. The idea of being a man now, I think, 'What a ghastly idea!' Sometimes I have to pinch myself; sometimes I think I'm going to wake up and I'm going to be a geezer again. Perish the thought!'

# 5

# Upright

Christina, 42, Surrey

*'I'm meant to be morally principled'*

'It came out in a big argument. I remember screaming, '*Why* haven't you asked me to marry you?' And Jim screamed back at me, 'Because we're not fucking having sex!' That pulled me up really short because he was right. That was the first time that one of us had said it out loud in an otherwise perfect – in inverted commas – relationship. The denial was popped.

We started to see a psychosexual counsellor and what we established was that I had a lot of physical pain during intercourse. When Jim and I would be having sex, when his willy was banging against me, I would have this pain in my womb which felt like somebody was pushing something too hard inside of me and I'd be going, '*Ow! ow! ow!*' I remember putting up with it, I would just lie there and let it happen, thinking, 'It feels like he's hurting me – it feels like I have to be passive in this, otherwise he's going to get upset.'

The counsellor suggested I get checked out medically. I go for the results to the gynaecologist and she said, 'There isn't *any* indication of endometriosis, which would be the first thing we consider, but I've got to tell you, Christina, most of the women who come to see me who've got pain during intercourse and who don't have a physical complaint have usually suffered abuse from their father. And had an abusive – not necessarily sexual – scenario caused by the father in the home of the young girl.' Which I'd never heard of before. And of course my dad was abusive in that there was a lot of physical violence that sometimes me and my sister would get on the wrong end of. Things would be thrown, doors would be slammed, walls would be punched, you know: rage. It was explained to me by my counsellor that an orgasm for men can be very similar to rage, in that there is a loss of control. Perhaps I was responding unconsciously to the loss of control element of intercourse, in the same way I used to respond to my dad, so it wasn't a pleasurable experience.

We then had to do this thing called touching exercises. Sex was banned. We had to make an evening whereby we would touch each other naked. This was before our daughter was born so that made things somewhat easier. First of all it's not even on your boobs or your bum or your bits – it's completely avoiding all of those sexy bits – just legs or hands or feet or hair or things like that. Then you build up to your erogenous zones. But I found myself in the bath once and Jim said, 'Are we going to do touching exercises tonight?' We've got a blunt knife in the bathroom because our sink plug doesn't open. I had this little knife in my hand. I went, *'Just don't! Just stop! Don't ask me. Just stop going on about it!'* I looked at myself with this knife; I couldn't be making more defensive gestures about the fact that I didn't want to be intimate. To be in that space was too hard for me. No wonder I was avoiding having sex, no wonder he felt rejected, no wonder all that stuff was going on.

Ironically, Jim went and had an affair. Unsurprisingly. It's rejection, isn't it? I was rejecting him constantly on a sexual level: 'I don't want you, I don't need you, I don't desire you, I don't want to know.' So what happens is that he goes off and finds that intimacy from somebody else. He left me for a week. Fortunately we were seeing our counsellor and he came back. But I thought he'd gone. I thought that was it. And that would have been a real shame: that the exposure to my dad's temper when I was little had had such wide-reaching and profound effects on my ability to be in an intimate relationship. Me and Jim have reconciled but it's taken a lot of work, a lot of commitment, and constantly having to go through the discomfort of looking at that side of our relationship, which we'd rather ignore, because who wants to look at the shitty bits? But it makes me sad when I think of other couples that haven't got to the bottom of what all that's about. So *thank* God Jim screamed in my face, '*Because we're not having sex!*'

I do have sexual fantasies. Mostly they're fantasising about being a stripper in a nightclub – those hideous, dingy clubs in Soho. I would look like those typical porn women, with porny-type underwear, so I wouldn't look like me. Or I have sexual fantasies about rape. I'd be in a club and let men have sex with me. They would absolutely sexually desire me. *Absolutely*. I would be an object of desire. The men would say the most horrendous things like 'You're going to love it, fucking whore' – like you see on films where men are raping women, and they'd say the most disgusting, hideous things. I would be raped by a whole line of men. A line of them! Loads. All different – not ones I find attractive: fat, bald, sweaty, dirty, horrible men. Anyone. Oh yeah! The point in the rape fantasy would be that I didn't get to choose. It's the whole notion of being powerless that is sexually exciting. It's submissive really, isn't it? I've gone back to that fantasy again and again. For years.

I'm meant to be morally principled and politically aware and for the right and for the greater good. Because my dad had a difficulty controlling his temper when we were growing up, if I even detect male oppression, I'm going to have a shit-fit irrespective of how that's going to make anyone else feel. So maybe there's a bit of childhood stuff going on in these inter-actions as well, I'm sure there probably is. I was listening to Radio 5 this morning and they were having a debate about sexual harassment in the workplace and this man called up and was amazed a male employee would no longer work for him because he'd tapped his employee's wife on her bum at the Christmas party. I was shouting at the radio, 'How dare you touch a woman's bottom, bum, backside? That's like touching her breasts. You don't touch people's breasts or their bottoms if you're not having a sexual relationship. That is a gesture to suggest, 'Are you up for it?' Sorry, but it is. Yet in my sexual fantasy I'm playing out what would happen with that bloke who touched his employee's wife – I'd let him have sex with me. I'd do that thing that I absolutely hate. I hate oppression. I hate somebody thinking they can do what they want without my consent – hate, hate, hate, hate, hate – and that's what I'm using as a sexual fantasy.

That's like my dark side, isn't it? It's like my shadow self that is the realm of my sexual fantasy. I have to conjure up scenarios where I'm effectively a prostitute. This isn't what I politically think – but then maybe the whole point about sexual fantasies is they're about archetypes, they're not about reality. It's almost as if I have to be the negative version of

46

myself in order to enjoy sex. My sexual fantasy is absolutely what I would abhor in normal life. It's like a negative of my conscious life.

In my sexual life with my husband everything is consensual. Yeah. Yes, yes, yes, yes, yes. But my sexual fantasies are the opposite of that: it's public, it's non-consensual, it's unprotected, it's dangerous, no one cares, I'm objectified, it's not married sex. It's not in a relationship. It's paid for. It's not free. It's a job, *no one* cares. I'm objectified. I'm not married, not in a relationship. It's abhorrent, actually. This is the shit that I have a sexual fantasy about.

I used to suffer from panic attacks. When I was five, my dad kicked me when I was on the floor, and I remember being pulled up off the carpet with my face really close to the carpet. My mum was there and she couldn't do anything because my dad was in a rage and I remember feeling, 'I'm fucked. He's not in control, she's not in control, who's in fucking control? No one's in control. I am at the whim of this man.' I've turned this abject horror and terror of dying into this sexual playground in which I dance and jump and skip and I love it, you know. It's like my psyche dumps all that shit and fear into this sexual bin and then the fear of that shit is exciting. You can't say, 'I'm five, I'm not going to dump that into my sexual fantasy pot.' It's happening unconsciously. And we're talking about the sexual drive, which is second only to the drive to stay alive; that's what I've heard.

I wonder if other people act out their fantasies of prostitution because they like feeling dirty? I would never do that, it would *never* occur to me to do that. I'm not being judgmental; I'm just saying that the fucking lid is shut really tight on that. I wouldn't act out my fantasies with my husband. *No. No!* My fantasy is an extremely private affair. I know this man extremely well, I'm forty-two, we've been together since I was twenty-nine and he was twenty-four; I have not told him about the line of men having sex with me. Or me being some dirty whore in some nightclub, letting anybody do what they want. I'd be embarrassed, I'd be exposed, I'd be vulnerable. I'd be in danger – bearing in mind I know that Jim wouldn't hurt me. It's bringing it into the light, then showing somebody, which is a risk. It's like showing somebody your dirty knickers, isn't it? Why would you show somebody you love the dredges of your psyche? Because he might judge? Because I'd feel shame? Would he think less of me?

I don't have any desire to act out my fantasy. But maybe that's part of my fucking problem in terms of my avoidance of sex. Maybe I could act a bit of my fantasies out, maybe I could bring some of that stuff into the bedroom with my husband, who's up for it. If I brought it into the bedroom with my husband whom I love and trust, and vice versa, maybe that would be a way of healthily incorporating that into our sex life. I don't know. Oh my God!'

# 6

# Lesbian

Paula, 53, south London

*'Vaginas are like flowers'*

'When I was fifteen I had my first relationship with a cousin. I knew it was wrong because I was having sexual feelings and being intimate with my cousin. I didn't think anyone would approve because she was female. People in the family knew but it wasn't spoken about. That was my first encounter of a same-sex relationship. And it was based on trust, love, warmth, comfort.

I'm the oldest of nine children, five to my mother and four to my father. Having been sexually abused from when I was six years old to aged ten by my mother's husband and his friend, for those four years I lived my childhood thinking I would be pregnant: didn't really know how you got pregnant but I was just terrified of being pregnant. It made me feel very ugly and I couldn't smile. People would say, 'Why does she never smile?' I had this thing going on in my life that no one saw.

My childhood shaped a lot of the choices I've made. I remember thinking, 'I don't want to be like my mum who tolerates a husband that has relationships with lots of other women and who is not considered good enough for him' – because that's what her husband thought. And I didn't want to be like some of my aunts and my cousins in the West Indies because they accepted what men did to them. They'd say things like, 'Well, that's what men do: they all play away from home. They come back to die. Or when they're not well. Or they come back when things are not okay out there.' I was really determined to not have that kind of relationship, or allow anyone to have that kind of relationship with me.

I remember having a boyfriend when I was sixteen and that felt like my choice. He was the boy next door. I wasn't allowed to be alone with him. My mother's new partner was really, really against it. He wanted me to have a relationship with his son, which felt so incestuous – more incestuous than me having a relationship with my cousin because that felt right. But this was like way serious – we lived in the same house. I had to stop having my relationship with the boy next door. He was absolutely besotted with me, he was lovely, he was a gentleman. I can't say anything wrong about him. He came from a more normal kind of family where women were treated differently. He was really brilliant and he went on to be the father of my daughter years later.

He was the first man I actively chose to have a sexual relationship with. And I couldn't satisfy him, because I couldn't take him, no matter how much I loved him. It was really painful physically as my womb had been damaged and tilted backwards from what happened as a child. I had pelvic inflammatory disease caused by the sexual abuse, but no one ever questioned why.

He was my best friend for years and during our friendship/relationship he stopped and had relationships with other people and that was fine, and I did too. Then when he realised I was having relationships with women he was so shocked, he was horrified – he felt that he couldn't compete. I found having relationships with women much easier, much better for me, but I still love men. I never saw myself as a lesbian. I wouldn't call myself a lesbian – I love men. But as I discovered sex and my sexuality, I found men unsatisfying.

We didn't have sex for eight months from June to February – then on Valentine's Day 1991, I remember cooking a Valentine's meal and making it really pleasant and then I got pregnant, after not having sex for eight months. I was like: 'Oh. My. God. What have I done?' I didn't want to get pregnant. No, no. But he wanted me to be pregnant so we went to counselling to work out whether or not we could work. I thought I could make him promise that I wouldn't be a single parent, which he promised, and then the trust came. I never wanted to be a single parent, having been the product of a broken relationship.

He would go to the local antenatal classes in Balham; I'd wait outside: I couldn't cope with these women who were perfect and pregnant. For seven months it was painful being pregnant. I lost weight, I felt as if I had a leech inside of me, it didn't feel like something was growing that was positive – I didn't feel any of that. I did not enjoy any of it. I booked my termination at St George's Hospital and attended three counselling sessions prior to it but he wanted this baby more than I did, more than anything, and I didn't have the heart not to do it.

During the pregnancy he wouldn't touch me in case I miscarried again. I'd lost a child: the child was with him. I'd miscarried because my womb was tilted in the wrong way. But I wanted to have wild sex and I felt the most sexual I'd ever felt. A friend of mine offered to have sex with me at the time and I said, 'Are you mad?' I couldn't believe he would say this, and, you know, I really wish I had! But I was being Miss Goody Two-Shoes and thinking, 'I can't possibly do that. How can I have sex with somebody else when I'm pregnant?' But it was what I wanted more than anything. I probably masturbated more when I was pregnant than at any other time in my life because I really felt sexy. I wanted to feel desired and I wasn't. I wanted to be touched and touched so deeply, to have penetration – but he – you know – was absolutely terrified in case I came and miscarried.

We went on and had the child and within a year he'd had an affair with somebody and that level of betrayal hit me like a bolt from the past – the deceit, the broken promises, the abuse of trust. He really tried to be supportive but I was just waiting for him to do what he was going to do and he did – he had an affair. Everything I feared he might do he did. It was almost as if I'd focused so much on what I didn't want that I created it. I didn't want to be a single parent, and what did I do? I became a single parent.

What I did eventually was I joined a women's group. It was a bit of an awakening for me. I was the only black woman and I was the youngest but the women's group was an opportunity to talk about sex and intimacy that I'd never had with my friends, my mum, the women in my life; it wasn't something they spoke about. I learned a lot with those women in that group. I was so prudey about stuff; I'd listen and think, 'Oh, that's not very nice,' and, 'How can you do that?' There was a sixty-year-old white woman and I really admired her. Some of the things she said I thought, 'I want to be like you, fully self-expressed sexually and emotionally and I don't want to hurt anybody but I want to be accepted for who I am and what I need.'

Through doing the homework, going into sex shops, looking at pornography from a different perspective and letting go of the prudishness I had, I learned about my own sexuality, and how to pleasure myself – and it wasn't dirty, it wasn't disgusting to think about satisfying my sexual desire. What I found out about fantasy is that it's normal; that it's healthy, and that there was a space where I could talk about it and I hadn't known where that space was – because it's taboo in certain circles.

We talked about our fantasies in the group and I began to share them with friends outside of the group. A lot of women think talking about fantasies is talking about male fantasies and they would talk about their partner's fantasy of them: what their partners wanted. But I was like, 'No, what about you? What do you want? This is what I want.' And it became normal that I could talk about fantasies with certain people. Even today I need to remember that I should probably interview any lover I have in the future because they need to like feet, they need to have strong hands, and they need to want to massage me. They need to want to touch me.

I used to have a fantasy about having sex with more than one person at the same time. It would be with a man and a woman and it would be equal. Then I would tussle with the idea; how can it *possibly* be equal? Or I'd have a fantasy where two people would be pleasuring me. I used to think that would be so selfish if I took all the pleasure. Then I had a relation-ship with a woman in Amsterdam who did *not* allow me to touch her intimately. Her body was very boyish and I've always been very voluptuous – this is the biggest I've ever been – I've always had boobs. I was really fit and I attracted a particular type of person. She would pleasure me. It was amazing. It was her sexual fantasy that she was living out. She would talk about the things she would like to do, talk about the things her friends did, and so it goes on and on and on, all these different fantasies. It was almost like I was benefiting from all the fantasies she'd had, that she'd shared with others. But she wouldn't let me pleasure her. I used to think that was so weird. It went on for five years. Sometimes now I miss that I could just be and she would enjoy thoroughly pleasuring me. It was totally one-way. So my fantasy came true. When I would be putting on my clothes afterwards, I'd think, 'Did that really just happen? But she's such a lovely woman, all she wants to do is pleasure me.'

I had a relationship with a woman who was married. She thoroughly enjoyed me pleasuring her: it became the opposite fantasy. I had these relationships through the eighties, interesting relationships, which I never really spoke about. Everyone assumed I was straight; it was keeping up appearances. My mother knew but it wasn't something she spoke about. I have had sex with a man with another girl there. I've slept with more black men than I have white men, so three black men and one white man, and there's no difference between them at all. But as I discovered sex and sexuality I found men unsatisfying.

A lot of women choose not to have sex with men, in my experience, because of the emotional and mental control men can display, even extremely passive men: it's that whole passive/aggressive behaviour you can get from a man when a man's having sex with you. Occasionally I miss having sex with men and if I do I might use a dildo, but not a vibrator because I don't like the vibrations. I don't like penetration.

I wouldn't think, 'Oh, I really want to be penetrated.' But if I was in the middle of having sex or having an orgasm I might allow them to penetrate me. I went for years without any penetration, and having relationships with women that weren't penetrative. Whereas I know lesbian women who have to be penetrated.

I've had sexual relationships with women where penetration with a strap-on dildo was absolutely important. I wanted to be penetrated by a woman; I wanted to have a woman make love to me. It feels *completely* different with a woman. There are women who fuck like men and want to fuck you hard to satisfy themselves. They feel sexually rough and won't hold you gently – I won't have a relationship with women who act like men. And there are women who penetrate you and make love to you really, really gently. A woman knows how to touch you and her skin feels different. It really does. I love being held by a woman. Being held by a woman is very different from being held by a man. It's warm and it's soft and it feels delicate. The thing that gives me an orgasm is being touched, being felt, the warmth of the breath, someone holding and talking to me.

Vaginas look different. Do you know the iris, the purple flower? And the orchid? There are loads of different orchids. Vaginas are like flowers. They all have different petals. That's absolutely true. In the women's group we had to look at each other's vaginas. When you look at a vagina, you see the labia – the outer flap bits – and they are all different. I've never seen two vaginas that look the same. Some vaginas have more flesh, some have less, some are fat, some are thin. It can be taut. And when you have an orgasm they swell up. And there is definitely a G-spot. I get used to a certain vagina. When I'm intimate with someone I really like, I don't see ugly and beauty, I see vagina.

55

All women smell different from each other. They taste different. Women's vaginas feel different – some are wet, some are dry, some are sticky. They're not sticky because they're dirty; they're sticky because their lubricant is sticky. They change as well. When you put on weight they change, because you get fat around your vagina, on your labia. I've always had a fat vagina. Even when I was skinny, I had a fat vagina. And a vagina can be closed, or can stay open all the time so it's like a hole. Those purple irises are a real good example of how vaginas look.

Some women really like to be eaten – for you to eat and play with their vagina with your mouth. Others want you to play with their clitoris or play with their labia. The clitoris sticks out, so sometimes there's a helmet over it which you pull down or back. Different women want to be touched in different ways so some people like being twisted, played with, being pulled back, being exposed, or being covered; it's about treating someone else in the way you'd like to be pleasured. And finding out if they want it or not. You don't ask, you explore.

People come in different ways so some women come really creamy and some women come really runny. Women have a discharge; other women are very, very wet like a tap – like men have sperm and ejaculate – and come a lot. We ejaculate in the vagina and sometimes it can spurt out of a woman, or it can come out like a flood, like a splash. They can come thick. It can be thin, it can be gooey, it can be creamy. Some women are extra wet; it's almost like they ejaculate. We ejaculate. We are no different from men.

What women do after they've had an orgasm is so different to what men do – men roll over, fall asleep and snore: they can't do any more: it's almost as if a man is so worn out with nothing left. When a woman's had an orgasm she starts all over again. It's so nice because it's the touching, it's the talking, it's the caressing: it continues. You don't feel like you're on your own after you've had an orgasm. We don't fall asleep. Might get up, get something to eat and start all over again.

I've been with my partner for over ten years, we've been living together for the last two and she's moving out at the weekend. In the last two years we've hardly had sex because the attraction's gone. Having sex will only happen if we talk about our fantasies or look at pornography. We can look at both male and female films but we probably look at lesbian films more because that turns her on and then she might soften, and I'll talk to her. We've gone from being in each other's skin – not going to work, being late, cancelling days out, so as to have sex – to not having sex. I know that happens in all relationships but it's not what I want for myself. I don't think we meet each other's needs any more in a lot of ways, and I'm ready to give up. I'm willing to go through missing her, losing her and letting go of the past. I don't want to be a hostage to the past. I don't want to be a hostage to 'what if …?' I'd rather let go.

I'm fifty-three. I've had lots of my fantasies fulfilled. I probably have some that are unfulfilled and I'd like to give myself time to think about new ones. I want to have fantasies because I don't want my sexual relationship with myself or anyone else to die. I want to be able to share my fantasies because I'm adventurous with intimacy and sexual relationships.'

# 7

# Explode

Jackie, 47, Eastbourne

*'Sometimes I would sleep with ten men a day'*

'When I met my child's dad, Sensible Steven, I was absolutely a hundred per cent sure I could love him. He was such a lovely man and I had it all worked out because he was clever, tall and he enjoyed drink and drugs like me and I decided he would be perfect to be the father of my child. Some months later I had my child. It lasted about a year and I couldn't love him, he repulsed me: he was very naïve sexually and sex for me is easy. I can do sex like that – not with emotion, just the act of sex; I like it, I'm good at it. What I showed him was this incredible sexual energy that he thought was love. I ruined him. That's when I stopped trying to love men because I knew that I couldn't. So I went off on one sexually – whoopee! I kind of exploded.

I found this guy in Kingston whose wife had left him. Ha. Called Gary. And I lived and worked in a pub with my child and this guy Gary. He was a very straight-looking man. We had sex sometimes, but we weren't a couple because I didn't want to be a couple with anyone because I wanted to have sex with lots of people. That was, I suppose, my fantasy, that I could just fuck everything. So. Anyway. One day he asked me to look under the bed and I opened the suitcase and there were all these handcuffs and women's stockings and he – bless him – was like, 'My wife didn't understand about this kind of stuff.' I was up for trying it out because it interested me to explore avenues that I wouldn't normally go down. Then by this weird coincidence these people came to the pub one Friday and they were all wearing long jackets and they were only going to Whiplash, which is an underground fetish club, and they invited me and Gary to go. We ended up in this club and I really liked it in that I'm quite controlling and I liked the power. And Gary was really quite submissive.

At the beginning Gary would wear women's underwear in bed. Then as time went on – bearing in mind we were doing quite a lot of drugs which makes it easier to explore your sexuality without caring – he would wear stockings under his clothes during the day; he'd cross his leg and I'd see his stocking underneath his suit or mannish trousers – stuff like that, and he'd be wearing a camisole under his shirt. This went on and on and I really liked it. I would chain him to the bed and leave him there and let people from the pub come upstairs to the flat – but not quite make it to the bedroom. He obviously couldn't move and so the thought of him being discovered would excite me. And him. We were never a couple; we had separate rooms but we used to act out these things.

Then we got this other pub and it had this huge bedroom and we put manacles on the wall. It was like scaffolding with massive chains from building sites hanging from the ceiling, not your fluffy handcuff things. He would wear women's underwear and I would chain him to the bed then I'd go down into the pub on a Saturday night and I'd pick a customer to fuck and I'd bring him up to the bed and I'd fuck him next to Gary who would be chained up in the same room – right next to him – so he wouldn't be able to move. Then obviously I'd fuck Gary as well. So that was quite cool. That went on for quite a long time. We had quite a good time doing that. And we didn't harm anyone: I mean, everyone was up for it. I liked the power and I liked him being vulnerable. He loved it too. In fact, he took it to a whole new level by dressing as a woman, which I didn't like. I came up from the bar one night and he was dressed as a woman and wanted to have a curry. That wasn't my fantasy. That was just weird. I was like, 'That's just weird, Gary,' and he was like, 'Okay.' 'You have to do that one with someone else. I don't want to eat a curry with you in a skirt. It looks like it's from C&A.'

After Gary, I met my husband. When I met my husband he was a rent boy – he was very sexy. Gary was still one of my best friends and he now had a girlfriend called Helen and we all used to sleep together but Helen wouldn't fuck my husband and I wouldn't fuck Gary but we'd all get off with each other and Gary would dress in women's underwear and my husband didn't give a fuck – he was sexy. We were a close-knit foursome, it just so happened we enjoyed being in bed together. They stayed in my bed on my wedding night and it seemed normal to me.

With my husband, I don't think we got out of bed for a year; well, we did, to go to work and take my child to school, but we spent *a lot* of time in bed, and not just having sex. That was loving, that was cool. Then we would go out and have fun sex. We had sex on the floor in the Electric Ballroom in

Camden Town on my wedding night – we got thrown out. I was wearing a black patent-leather PVC dress and fishnets; it was one of my better outfits. And I loved my husband. I hadn't loved a man till I met my husband. But then he killed himself. So. I kind of thought I deserved that because of my childhood, which was wrong. My thinking was weird.

After he died I went on a fucking spree. Ha. Once my child had gone to live with their dad I went into a bit of free fall: drugs and alcohol, and sexually. My fantasy then was ... well, I put an advert on Gumtree saying '*Loves to dance, loves to laugh, loves to ...*' It was clear it was '*fuck*'. And within four hours I had four hundred hits.

I put what I was looking for: '*No sympathy fucks.*' I only fuck fit men – I don't fuck ugly men because it's my fantasy, isn't it? I wouldn't care how old they were; I'm not an ageist or racist – I have no judgment on that, I'm completely open – but they had to have a certain look because it's sex and I don't want to have sex with someone I don't find attractive. I have done as a prostitute but that's not the fantasy at all. They had to be skinny, fit and tall and have a big dick: a slightly above average size dick or bigger. This is sex so of course I would like to have a fair-size cock to have sex with, so I needed to ask them, 'How big is your cock?' If they'd got a small cock then they must leave. If they were into drugs? If they were in a relationship? I wouldn't sleep with people's husbands: there are enough people in the world to sleep with. I wasn't trying to harm people's relationships. I only slept with other consenting couples or single people – or as far as I knew they were single. They said they were single – I didn't CV them. It's still an intimate act: you need to be fully armed with the facts before you go in – I'm a Virgo, very analytical. If they had their own flat? Because I'm too independent to be mollycoddling somebody; I don't want them to even stay for a cuddle after sex, never mind live with them.

I used to email them, then I would meet them in Richmond Park which was a nice place to spend the afternoon – they would normally do drugs like me, happy drugs – and then I would take them back to the gay couple's house: I was living with these two gay guys. Sometimes we'd make them parade round in their boxer shorts and the gay guys would check them out for me to make sure that they were up to scratch. If they weren't who they said they were they'd not a chance. Sometimes we'd all be on the bed together, gay guys doing gay stuff and blowjobbing and kissing and I would do the guy, depending on how open-minded he was. There are some beautiful men – yeah. And then I'd sleep with them and then they'd be off. I did that for the next five or six years.

Sometimes I would sleep with ten men in one day. I liked the repetitiveness of it. Made me feel powerful, to be honest. I used to have numbers in my phone as *Fuck 1, Fuck 2* or, if they were really fit, *Fit fuck*. It was practically a full-time job. I had sex on Victoria station – was it Victoria or Waterloo? I had sex in the rush hour under the stairwell on the platform and then we got on different trains – no one said anything. People could tell we were having sex: oh, yeah. Very quick sex, bent over. Then we just walked onto separate trains. That was cool. You can't go home and sit on the sofa after that kind of sex: I have to be sitting on the train thinking, 'Look what I just did! And didn't get caught.' It's like a hit from a drug.

I could sleep with any man I wanted to, probably. Men are easy. You just get your fuck strut on – that would make a great song, wouldn't it? *'Get your fuck strut on!'* Men are easy to manipulate. I come from posh but I was very manipulated; it was what I was taught as a child, to be manipulative as a survival instinct. If you give a man enough signals that you want to have sex with him ... To be fair, I could tell the men who didn't want to sleep with me and I wouldn't try. I'm quite a good judge of who and what I want, and if they'd want me back, because I don't like rejection: I've got a big ego. But I set quite high standards. Definitely wouldn't get rejected much – or not at all.

My friends all really laugh at me because I seem to be a good judge of if a man's got a big dick, because the man has an inner confidence if he's got a big dick. Men who have big cocks kind of know. We called one of my fuck buddies Max, because he had the biggest cock in the world, it was ridiculous. I don't think I could take it now. It was like a donkey's. It came up about three inches above his belly button. I'm not being funny. I would say it was on its way to ten inches, eleven inches long. It was a mad willy. It was the biggest one I'd ever had. And his nickname – his name was Timmy, for God sake – his nickname was Max because it was just so big. It was big when it was flaccid so it wasn't like a thing that grew. It was just huge. I think it might have hurt more if I hadn't taken a lot of drugs. We used to watch *Julius Caesar* on television in his bed and take drugs and fuck. He was beautiful as well.

I gave Max as a gift to my friend. Well, Max was my shag buddy for quite a while. And lying in bed watching films and having sex lasts a while but not forever because I want someone new to fuck. There's no emotion so after a while it's not as exciting; I get bored easily. And I had a friend who was lovely. It was a year after my husband died and we were at my house celebrating my husband's suicide anniversary and people were keeping me company. Max came and I said to him, 'I'm not that up for fucking you any more, go and fuck *her* – she'll enjoy it.' She was like, 'Do you really mean it?' and I said, 'Yes, go on!' And she did. Max was quite selfish in the end as a lover. Some men are lazy if they have a big cock.

I like giving pleasure to people. That's what it started as because it made me feel better about myself. I would see a man and I would think, 'I could give you a lot of pleasure. We could have some fun. And it will be all right.' And it would fix him for a little while. Men like to have their cocks sucked. There's a skill to blowjobs – I have that skill. Just think about lollypops: lick it and suck it and bite it. It's like an art form and it's a very powerful thing to be able to do because men love it, absolutely. I used to do it when I was a whore so I got really good at it. And I love doing it. I wouldn't use a condom when I gave a blowjob, but bearing in mind when I was using drugs I didn't really care. I had a hysterectomy when I was thirty-four and after that I had this attitude that nothing would affect me because there was nothing to infect. I don't have a cervix or anything, so my mad thinking was that it was just going into an empty hole so what would the infection cling to? I didn't get anything. And I don't get thrush. I don't know how I didn't get something. I wouldn't recommend that to anyone who does it.

I got more pleasure out of making them come. I didn't want much back. I was quite happy to give it away, then do it myself. I wouldn't let them make me come. I'd come in front of them but I'd do it. I was in control, absolutely. I don't think a man deserves my orgasm. And as much as I'm turned on, I can do it myself, and they can watch. I didn't take my clothes off in bed. Childhood: dirty. With my last shag buddy I did take my clothes off a few times but I'm very eager to put my clothes back on. It's because I can leave quicker and I don't really see why I should have to be naked: they don't really deserve it. I'm so controlling.

I love having sex and walking away. I find that really exciting. To finish and say, 'You can go now; I'm done.' Men always assume you're going to say, 'Oh, stay. Come back.' Men are surprised by women who want sex like that because men have this mad feeling that every woman's going to have the necessity for it to be repeated, or for there to be time spent together afterwards, or that you need to put words in it, or emotions other than sexual feeling. When a man's had sex with a woman he tends to think – well, I don't think they think; I think the animal takes over – he feels the need to protect her – you know – like animals do, or that she might be vulnerable after sex. Men do want to do that protectiveness, but I don't want it. It's just sex; it's not a possessive feeling.

More and more people began to come to my house; they came in hour-and-a-half slots and I discovered the money side of things. I'm good at business skills from running a pub – I just moved the skills around a bit. Little by little what happened was some people started to pay me, which was also quite cool; bearing in mind that my mind was pretty fucked up. Sex to me was just something that gave me power. At first it was like a donation thing. I would get up and the bloke would have left and I'd notice there'd be money on the side and I'd think, 'Oh, okay, they think I'm a whore. *Ha ha ha!* I'll do that. That sounds like a really sensible plan.' I did all right by accident. That was in the heydays, in the good days. I wasn't like, 'It's £30 pounds for this; it's £30 for that.' It would never be less than fifty quid.

Then I ended up going to offices in London to sleep with the directors of companies. I'd know them on the internet, and they'd say, 'Can you come at 2p.m.?' I'd just pretend I was some sort of marketing manager or something at the reception desk. When I was going to people's offices, I'd go up and shag them in their offices and they'd give me the money. I would just be walking in, fucking them and leaving them. I don't know if people knew, I don't think I cared. I wasn't doing anything wrong in my head. I used to think that was a *fucking* great thing to do.

I had great fun. I learned that it's all right to be like that. I learned to be comfortable with sex. I learned that people actually quite like having sex and having fun. Sex isn't a bad thing. I think sex is fine. It's how we make babies and how we fuse each other together. And there aren't many rules for sex. It would be more fun if people were more up for it. Isn't that everyone's fantasy, to be happy in bed and not feel inhibited? The only thing that came out of all that was I was hurting myself, but to be honest I wouldn't change anything that I did apart from one thing: I slept with one of the gay guys I was living with and I should never have done that because he was in a relationship and it really fucked it up. I mean, he was obviously not quite as gay as he thought; he was very up for it. It was the most harmful thing I've ever done in my sex life. It ended very badly and I had to leave the house and leave the husky dogs.

As I got more drunk and drugged it fell apart and I started to get psychosis and that spiralled into me being a prostitute on the street, which I quite enjoyed. I liked the power of it and the money. It was easy. It gave me the drugs I wanted. It was dirty and I felt dirty inside so it fed my dirtiness. And I was in free fall: my husband was dead, my child wasn't ... I still have no contact with my child. I didn't have much to live for, I suppose. With drink and drugs I didn't make a personal choice because I was addicted to it, but to be honest, with the sex thing I didn't have to do it and I wanted to. I wanted to prostitute myself on the streets. My truth was I liked it. So I did it.

When I got to the evil crack-whorey stage, I was fucked. I was using heroin and crack and living on the streets and I was poorly as well. But it wasn't damaging me; I was damaged already so I didn't find it 'Oh my God, I've got to go and do that' at all. I'd still prostitute myself quite happily – it's not a moral thing – but I know that doing stuff like that would stop me finding love. Not because I find being a prostitute bad, I still find it a *really* interesting life. What I miss most is that seediness, I like that seediness; sexually I find it exciting. My tattooist is really cool and when I go out with her for a night the draw of that life is huge.

No idea how many people I've slept with. Thousands? And then there are the ones I don't remember. I've met a few since I've got clean: there's been a few come to Eastbourne. There was a guy – I thought I'd had a one-night stand with him; apparently I was with him six months, but that was after my husband died and I was pretty fucked with post-traumatic stress disorder and on Valium, and Valium takes away your memory. I was, 'I remember you – we had a one-night stand!' And he was like, 'We went out together for six months. I left and went to treatment after that.' I was like, 'I remember you! You came into my pub, and I took you up to my flat and fucked you,' and I thought that was it! So yeah, that wasn't good for his ego.

In six years of being clean from drugs. I've only slept with five people: I've really changed. But I'm probably more outrageous and naughty when I'm not having sex because I'm thinking about it more so I tend to misbehave or swag it down the street a little bit more – but then again that's not true because I do it after sex as well because it feels powerful. I don't wear knickers. When I go out without a skirt on I definitely start swaggering – without having *knickers* on, I mean!

Very uplifting to not wear knickers because of the air, and it's sexy as well. I can think, 'They don't fucking know that I've got no knickers on,' and it's funny. And it's got a kick. I feel sexy even if I don't, in that moment, want to have sex. I still want the attention. I like people to look to me: a lot of people do anyway because I'm covered in tattoos and piercings.

Now my fantasy would be to fall in love. I didn't know when I got clean that I might want a relationship with someone again, but clearly I do. My mind and body are healing, despite myself, even if I don't want them to. Recently I decided I'm having a sex ban because if I keep having casual sex that's what I'm going to have for the rest of my life. Having casual sex stops me learning to love someone again because I can fix myself on casual sex really easily for that moment. I don't walk away thinking, 'Oh no, I've got to text this person.' Only, when a man touches me affectionately I don't know what to do, it makes me feel so uneasy. But I desperately want a cuddle. When I see people who are lovingly in love with each other and they want to talk to each other as well – I don't really get that because the person I loved killed himself so ... Then from my childhood the love was fucked up anyway.

I'd probably still want an open relationship sexually, because jealousy isn't my thing, weirdly. My husband was a very beautiful man but he was possessive over me. I wouldn't have slept with anyone else without him there: you have to have rules and boundaries. If you love someone, you trust them and you do everything together, like me and my husband did. I don't want the same thing as I had before; that would be like trying to replace it. I'd want a similar sort of thing but I don't want them to kill themselves. I don't want it to come with the fucked-up-ness. I want someone who's open-minded but I also want someone who makes me feel safe; it's quite tiring being independent and fiercely sexual. My fantasy is to love again. Which is a bit boring really; but I suppose not if you haven't been loved. Now my fantasy is for love.

Part of my fantasy would be that I'd feel safe enough to let go of my control. That would be scary, wouldn't it? Nowadays I want someone to take control even though I don't like it. My fantasy would be to hold hands in public with someone and then have sex with him. I'm going to grow daisy chains, aren't I? I'm going to go from being a hardcore prostitute to holding someone's hand. Imagine the poor man – or poor woman – who has to deal with that!

I would shag for a good dick, oh ... the chef at the hostel I'm staying at. Oh, I want to sleep with him. He's beautiful. He's called John, which was my husband's name, which is really bad. I've been really good: I haven't slept with him. He's going to 'rub me up' a burger tonight. That's how bad we're flirting. Instead of 'cooking me up a beefburger', for God's sake! Honestly! He wants to keep on hugging me and I'm like, 'Stop it, get down, *back!* You bad chef!' and all the young girls are giving me really, really bad looks because we're laughing and flirting. They looked surprised that he'd want to flirt with me because I'm forty-seven but that's because they don't know – do they? – that I'm really good in bed. I know it. And he knows it, because I'm giving him that 'I'm-really-good-in-bed' nick.**'**

# 8

# Nun

Olive, 35, Leeds

*'It was laden with guilt, mixed with pleasure'*

'In my first year at uni, I was looking for meditation classes and I ended up in a Buddhist centre. I walked through the door and I thought, 'I'm home.' I carried on walking through the building and I saw a statue of the Buddha and I thought, 'I'm a Buddhist.' It was like love at first sight, it was a profound spiritual experience. I threw myself into that religion and I got ordained as a Buddhist nun within the year, and with that comes vows of celibacy. So I shut down my sexual self and I remember feeling the relief of, 'Thank goodness I don't have to deal with sex.' Partly I didn't know what I was missing because I'd never had sex. Also, I was twenty so I didn't have that sense of longevity and the future and, you know, life's different when you're twenty.

When I heard the teachings I got these magnificent visions and it was beyond reasoning and questioning. I saw a living Buddha, I saw lots of different forms of Buddhas. I had conversations with them. I had experiences of being in this completely pure world. Of the ground turning to gold and exotic creatures everywhere, and the trees laden with gems and magnificent birds. All interactions were based on love and compassion and patience and abundance, where everything flows and is smooth, and whatever you need appears. There was also this deep sense of peace within me; I got washed in a wave of love and compassion.

I'd just had a very horrific year with my parents' divorce; I'd had to testify against my dad for domestic violence. So it was very traumatic and dramatic. Also I was very lonely at uni. I had friends and I went out and partied but there weren't any deep connections. I came from a broken family and suddenly there was this whole family at the Buddhist Centre. I loved the value of people working together for a common goal rather than for themselves. And from a very young age I had had a deep yearning or thirst for spirituality and meaning. I was adamant that I had found a purpose in life. I wasn't running away. I was twenty so I knew everything! I do strongly believe if I hadn't gone down that path I would have gone down a much more destructive path of probably drugs and alcohol because I'm prone to extremes. So I threw myself into the extreme, into this spiritual path. It was a protection. Otherwise no doubt I would have ended up in violent, abusive relationships. But then having said that ...

I must admit I did feel very beautiful in the robes. There was a beauty to those magenta, maroon and yellow robes. People were drawn to the purity and spirituality they represented. I had a shaved head. That was completely asexualising. I didn't mourn my hair for one second. I had long brown hair and it was like, 'Get it all off!' It was a very liberating experience. And it did feel great when I got in the shower and I just came out. I liked being bald. I never felt overly self-conscious. I'd go out with a bald head. It's intended to be empowering, not disempowering, in that I was very definitely focused on a spiritual path so I've got no need for worldly things.

The Buddhist Centre was a mixed community of fifteen monks, nuns and lay practitioners – part of the philosophy is to integrate our beliefs into modern life rather than separating from ordinary life. Because I was very keen and I'm also a very capable person I was snapped up right away to do all of the organising of running a residential property. Very quickly I was asked to teach courses to the public and I was very popular as a meditation teacher. People really resonated with me; they just warmed to me.

The biggest issue is the people you live with. What came first was this sexuality with a teacher. It was a crush on a Buddhist teacher, and he was showing me pornography. On the Internet. All sorts, everything. There was nothing violent; well, I think most pornography is violent. He was doing it because that was what he was doing at the time. Things progress, don't they? You start watching funny clips on YouTube and then ... I wasn't cut off from the world. And he was very chauvinist. So it wasn't a very empowering experience of sexuality.

Then I had images and I had a visual of porn stars, of women with shaved pubic hair and that was when I started to explore that. I shaved all my pubic hair off. As part of being a nun. And it felt very wrong; it was all very confusing. You don't have to shave your pubic hair if you're a nun – it was an exploration. It felt dirty, unlike my shaved head. I thought, why am I doing this? I'm a nun. There was this natural sexual awakening that was taking place but also a feeling of guilt and shame. In hindsight I can see it was all tied up with guilt and shame from childhood. At the time I thought, oh it's because I'm a nun and that's why I feel so guilty and shameful. I had thrush so I got a pessary and I remember feeling really guilty because I enjoyed that. Again that was a sexual awakening of sorts, a sensation of ... I didn't masturbate for the first six years of being a nun and then it got progressive. Theoretically nuns are not supposed to masturbate because it's no sexual activity. But it's also the lesser of two evils so if masturbation is what will give your ordained life longevity then do it. To begin with I didn't even know how to masturbate, the physical action of what to do. Do I just touch myself? Do I stroke myself? Do I press?

I was asked to be a team principal teacher, which is where you have overall responsibility for the whole centre. I had a job of responsibility and I had status although it wasn't status in the conventional sense: I hadn't become an executive driving a Ferrari. I was respected and had a good reputation and was very popular. That's when it all imploded. And that was when I lost all my status.

This is something I don't talk about a lot, because that was when I got involved with, developed romantic feelings for, one of my friends, a male. I was absolutely convinced that I was dedicated to my path but then I met this person whom I connected with completely. It wasn't the pure physical attraction; we connected on our vulnerability, on the deepest level. He was a Buddhist monk. It was my first experience because I hadn't had any sexual experience, even before I got ordained. And it felt *completely* natural with him. And he was very tender. He was very sensitive as a sexual partner and also adventurous. And it was just effortless. It didn't feel sordid in any way; it felt very much a friendship that almost overnight turned. We had our own individual rooms at the Buddhist Centre and where there's a will there's a way, isn't there? It wasn't like it was planned. Up to that point I was wary of touch apart from with young children – I mean that in a very clean way. I didn't like people touching me. Yet with him I felt safe. It felt the most natural thing in the world. He was very experienced, and quite promiscuous before he became a monk. He was bisexual and he'd had a lot of varied experiences, and also there is that wild side in me, so it was very adventurous. We never actually had sex.

This all happened in the space of a few weeks and no one knew about it. It never got as far as thinking of leaving and living together, it was very much in that moment. He confessed but carried on living his life as a monk. I confessed because I wanted to stay a nun. I wanted to be true, authentic. Oh, I was devastated when I broke the vow. It was a beautiful experience, but nevertheless it was devastating to me. I felt shame at my own arrogance – 'I'm this spiritual person' – and that was a short slap in the face! I felt a lot of guilt because I thought I'd disrespected the path I was on. The impact I'd had on his spiritual life – I carried all the guilt and responsibility for that. I'd let people down who'd had faith in me. That sense of, oh, my whole life has imploded. A whole cauldron. I was fighting for my ordination.

I wasn't asked to stop being a nun but they said, 'Well, you can't be a teacher any more. After going on retreat, if you still want to teach, then ...' I went into silent retreat for nine months. So I didn't speak for nine months. It was in a retreat centre in Indonesia. That was a very profound experience. It taught me that life is life, no matter what the external is: even though I was in silence it was still me as a person living in a world. It was a different environment but it was still me.

I did notice my thoughts slowing down and having a real clarity and sharpness. I got used to the silence although there was still that continual conversation in my head. I thought I would feel lonely but it was the least lonely I'd ever felt. It's fascinating; the internal world is fascinating.

But there was incredible pain involved. In the last three months I thought, 'One possibility is I'm going to lose my mind completely! Just go insane.' That wasn't the case at all. But what did come up was all that emotion that had been pushed down from my childhood, and also from more recent years. I felt betrayed by my Buddhist centre because I had given up so much. I'd come from a wealthy background – I'm not saying it's about money – I was privately educated, I was all set for a career in psychology and a good life, a so-called good life, and I'd willingly given all that up and I was seeing more flaws in what I'd handed my life over to. I suffered from eating disorders when I was a teenager, and those symptoms started coming back again so I was eating a lot and I got to the point where I was making myself throw up and that was when I decided to stop doing the retreat because I thought, 'This is no longer good for me.' I was told to go on retreat for a year and I had accepted that. But then I made the decision, wisely or otherwise, to stop.

I moved back into a Buddhist centre and I got very ill and was in bed for a week: I couldn't eat, I couldn't drink, I couldn't move. That was when I got memories of sexual abuse. I got back in contact with the monk – because he was the only person that I trusted. Even though I hadn't spoken to him for two years he was completely there for me, as I knew he would be. When I went into retreat one of the conditions I placed was to have no contact with him; I had thought, let him get on with his life and me with mine.

He was living in a flat in Wales. So I moved there, and I had no notion that I didn't want to be a nun any more. Very quickly I had a breakdown that lasted a year and during that time the monk – his name is Andrew, he had a Buddhist name at the time – was there for me. He was there to listen, emotionally he was there, and also physically because I wasn't eating so he was cooking. He was getting me out of bed and driving me to my counselling sessions. I was still ordained and he was still a monk. It was during this time we resumed some kind of sexual relationship. Again, it was the old cliché – it just happened! It was laden with guilt, mixed with pleasure. That was the first time I questioned the whole basis of my ordination: had it been simply a reaction to past sexual abuse?

I had a fantastic counsellor; she helped me through it. I got back on my feet and was a lot stronger in myself. I even confronted my dad, who was the perpetrator. It was horrific. It was very painful. He denied it and he mocked me but it was also very liberating and empowering. The most painful side of it was my brother and my sister took my dad's side. My mum went into denial. My middle sister supported me. I've got no relationship with my father – I don't want anything to do with him.

A year ago I decided not to be a nun any more. All in all I was a nun for twelve years. When I was moving out I had nothing: I had no savings, I had no career. To walk away from the centre was to also not have food and board. I was suddenly back in Leeds without anywhere to live. I was doing domestic cleaning as a job, I rented a flat and got a second job in a wholefood shop, and I've been doing that for the past year. Then before the summer my mum said, 'I want to help you,' so she bought a property in Leeds which I've just moved into.

It's a very gradual process of pulling away the layers of

being a nun. Incredibly painful to leave and I still have times when I mourn that person and that life. This past year has been about me very openly exploring my womanhood. It took me two months after – we call it derobing – to register, 'Oh, I can actually wear make-up now and more feminine clothes.' It was the opposite of what I had been trying to be as a nun when I was always very modest and I tried not to be too sexual. Growing my hair has been a very courageous move on my part because I'm saying sexuality and sexual contact is now a definite possibility whereas before, at least theoretically, it was not – and I had a very valid reason – 'Oh, I'm a nun! No!' I feel like I'm going on my journey with my hair because we're growing together. I went through a phase where I looked like a little fluffy chicken. It felt symbolic. I want to grow my hair really long and then decide what shape it takes. That's something else I've had to get used to: allocating time to dry my hair.

Andrew's not going through a good time, he's smoking a lot of pot and that's consumed his life and he's gone downhill. He decided he didn't want to be a monk any more, separately and nothing to do with me. It's been a very painful time in relation to Andrew because he's done a lot of push-and-pull with my emotions. He's broken my heart time and time again. Because he doesn't have any romantic feelings for me but he continues to put himself in those situations with me and being so loving and nurturing and sensitive, yet saying, 'But we're just friends.' We haven't had much sexual contact for a year – ironically since neither of us are a monk or a nun. That was when our sex life stopped

Very strangely, I now wish we had had sex. We did everything, basically. We did come very close and then I stopped it. There's a part of me that wishes I hadn't let fear hold me back but then there's another part of me that says, 'Well, I had to honour myself too.' Being sexual was so powerful for me, and such a turning point. I said that to Andrew: 'You know, even though the circumstances were awful, each experience sexually I had with you was very healing.' Because I had every reaction – I had ecstasy, I had guilt, shame, I had tears, I had sadness – and I was able to express all of that freely with him. The very fact that I was being sexual with someone was so healing.

I fantasise now. Recently, since I've not been a nun, I bought a vibrator and I've used that a few times and I enjoy that. And with Andrew, even though we didn't have sex, he would put his hand inside me, and that felt really nice and I really enjoyed that. But for a long time I had a big mental block about having anyone's penis inside me, and that is because of the sexual abuse. It took months and months of being with Andrew to feel, 'I would actually have sex with you,' but at that point he was like, 'I don't feel that way about you.' So that was quite heartbreaking. I've hidden from genuine experiences through having this half-fantasy, half-real relationship with him. It's kept my emotions tied and my thoughts tied and been another way of creating a block to actually having that sexual experience.

I know I'm a deeply sexual person, I use the word *sexual* in the broadest sense: I'm sensual, I'm passionate, I'm creative, I'm tactile, so there's a lot in there to be exposed, but I feel it's blocked. I'm only sexually active with myself. I masturbate most days, morning and evening, and that's quite a lot and sounds like there's something in me that needs to be expressed. I feel frustrated. I think, what is the point of having this incredible energy inside me that's not being expressed in relation to others? It's often fantasies that really get me going. A lot of times it's me on top being in my full power. Sometimes the fantasies will be with a man, imagining a very sensual experience with him on top and me underneath and being completely taken over. Sometimes it's two men having sex with me. I wish it was a reality, not a fantasy; it would just be great! How wonderful it would be. I do have this wild streak. I really enjoy giving blowjobs; often my fantasies start with that. Sometimes what really gets me going are fantasies involving other women or other women orgasming.

I do feel curious to know what sex feels like. More than anything I want to get it out of the way. So it's no longer a big deal. And I question, what is it in me that's blocking it? It does feel like a big deal. My fantasy earlier on this year was, 'I'm going to find a soul mate who I'll have sex with.' Now I think someone with whom there's mutual respect; that will do me. Even if it's a one-night stand, even if it's a short-term fling, as long as for that moment in time there's mutual respect. It doesn't have to be a big romantic thing. Another deep insecurity I have is, where on earth am I going to find a sexual partner? Who is prepared to deal with the fact that I'm a thirty-five-year-old woman who hasn't had sex, who's got a traumatic background? I think, 'Who wants to take that on?' I know from male friends that they think, '*Oh my God!* That's like someone's world of fantasy!' So there's probably something in between that is healthy. I'd love to have a life partner to share the burden of responsibility. Someone to take care of me, and look after me. I really want to be a mother, to birth a child. I almost think I want a child so much that I don't know if I'll have one.

I was very clear when I decided not to be a nun why I was doing it. I wanted to explore being a woman and to step into womanhood. As a young girl I always had *incredible* respect for women and I have this deep respect for women and what women can do. There is a real power in womanhood and in the feminine. There's something very powerful about the womb itself and I'm reclaiming the innate power that is in every woman. I love men as well, I believe in equality and equal rights, so I'm not talking about raising women above men. Nevertheless, I felt like there is a real deep knowing and knowledge and strength in being a woman.'

# 9

# Modern

Lola, 23, Essex

*'I was trying to find the best phone app if you want casual sex'*

'My dad, he gets on my nerves. He's very shouty. Indian men, they don't think, they shout at you. He's not like a cuddly dad. I'm telling you, we go for men that are like our father; that's what I believe. My dad's a bit – I'm going to say it straight – he's a bit of an arsehole – he's got arsehole-olic tendencies, so I don't think I've had a positive start with men. My sister did a self-esteem course and this woman who runs it, she told my sister, 'You go after men who are like your father. It's something that we do. Sometimes you seek love from a source that you can't get love from.' You always fight for your dad's love and that's what you do with other men. Me and my sister were discussing why we've never had nice men in our life and maybe it's down to our father, who knows? My sister and me, it wasn't really in our destiny to have nice boyfriends, growing up.

I've just finished university and I'm working in Selfridges

at the weekend, and I live with my dad, who's a warehouse operator, and my sister. Our mum died in 2008 when I was seventeen. I was quite vulnerable then in terms of guys, I was kind of taken advantage of once or twice. I've had sexual intimacy with a guy but I've never had a boyfriend. But I was sexually active when I was fifteen! On Blackberry Messenger there was this boy called Alan or something; I liked him. He was seventeen; I just lied about my age. I didn't know him at all. I went to his house – he lived far away – and that's the first time I had a kiss from a guy. Then he wanted to do more stuff and I was like, 'No, I can't, I don't want to.'

I went to his house again the following week and he showed me his penis. I thought we were going to have sex and he goes, 'Oh, you're too tight. You're a virgin so I'm not going to do anything, but practise on yourself.' So I practised on myself. I didn't meet him again, I didn't want to do it with him, I didn't like him. He wasn't very nice. He used to text me racist things like 'Paki'.

I never saw him again but I still wanted to do it, so there was this other guy, Marvin. He didn't go to my school. He was someone I met on Blackberry Messenger. I'd heard stuff about him so I went to his house and lost my virginity when I was fifteen. I didn't know him! I don't know what was going on: my mum had cancer at the time so maybe something happened there that turned on my brain. It was really good – the sex. It hurt at first, but it was really good. So my first time wasn't bad. I've had intercourse twice since. Nothing has quite been the same as that.

The next time – another random guy. This was a guy called Lee. I met him in a club – this was two years ago – and then we were texting and he was in the same club as me a month later. And I was really, really drunk so I ended up going back with him to the hotel room where he was staying. He worked in the hotel so he got a discount on the rooms. I was with Lee in the toilet, and his friend was in the next room waiting – and we were in the toilet having sex. It's one of the trashiest things, I think. What happened was he took me to the toilet, I was against the wall and I think he was doing it up my bum. He goes, 'I want to doggy you.' I was too drunk to even say no. So I did that with him.

I remember lying down with Lee afterwards. I really liked this guy, I didn't know him that well – he was very good-looking. You know when you just look at someone? I started getting attached; I was staring at him. He was like, 'Stop staring at me, stop staring.' He knew women get attached. He was okay with me in the morning. He goes, 'Do you want to go for a McDonald's?' I said, 'I'm not hungry.'

Then we met up again the following week, I don't know why. He brought his friend along because his friend had nowhere to stay. I think they wanted a threesome. I started my period one hour before I was meant to meet him, so we couldn't really have sex. I told him, and he wasn't very happy about that! He goes, 'Oh, that's fine, you're on your period, we can kiss all night.' I left for the bathroom, then his friend came in the room and I overheard him telling his friend, 'I'm really pissed off; she's on her period. And that's the one thing that really pisses me off.' We were just watching music channels in the hotel room, his friend was on one bed and me and Lee were on the other bed. I remember kissing him, I gave him a blowjob, we talked, and then the next day we had breakfast and that was that.

I was with my sister in Nando's a month later and I go, 'I met this boy, blah, blah, blah.' She was, 'Okay, that's fine, it's your life. Did you use a condom?' I was like, 'Er, I don't think he did.' She was like really angry. She was like, 'Delete him. Block him. Go and get an STD check.' When you like someone it's not always so easy to delete them. I got the STD check; that was fine. Yeah, Lee's very good-looking! I go for handsome player-types – yeah.

I have fantasies about Lee. It's weird; I wouldn't mind dressing up as a schoolgirl for him. I guess I would do anything he wants, actually. Certain things I wouldn't allow him to do. Like, no threesomes with his friends. No video recording. If we ever have sex again I don't want it to be when we're drunk or when I'm drunk. I want it to be when I'm sober. And no to anal sex with him, that's one thing I say no to. Anything else, I'd do it. Yeah.

My sexual fantasy is to dress up. Last year Christmastime I wanted to dress up in a Santa suit. You know you get the little red suit and a boob tube? That's my fantasy. I don't want to do it with any random guy any more. So I'm kind of waiting. I want a proper relationship where I can do it, because that's when I'm going to get the most out of it. I want Lee to go down on *me*! That's one thing I want. I'd like to try sixty-nine. I have a fantasy about my own body – I want my bum to be bigger! I have another fantasy, right: I've seen it in porn. When you're Asian or exotic-looking, I feel like white men look at you like some kind of exotic being. So I've had this fantasy; I'm lying down and I have a really big bum, so funny! And this white man comes in and I imagine him being American and then we have sex ... and I have a really big bum. He's like, 'That's a pretty good ass,' in an American accent. I think that's something to do with my subconscious – colonialism or something. Something else deeper is going on there. I imagine him being a bit older, he's a bit more experienced and I don't think he'd take his clothes off; he'd keep his T-shirt on.

I was reading *Fifty Shades of Grey*. And I think that's a good book. Everything was so la-di-da-di-da for Christian and Anastasia, it made me feel depressed in my own life. Although Christian does all that sadomasochist stuff, he really *cares* about Anastasia. Christian is the most handsome guy, a billionaire, he's nice but he's got that sadomasochism; that must have been a bit weird for Anastasia. The best part came when she started to really enjoy the sadomasochistic sex and there's a time when they're in a bathroom when he takes her razor and starts shaving her. It's good because there's that intimate kind of thing. I thought I would use *Fifty Shades of Grey* as a fantasy. So I had a fantasy where I work in a publishing house, like Anastasia, and this Christian Grey figure turns up. I thought publishing sounded nice – I get to wear all these nice skirts and blouses. We just stare at each other. He's an attractive character, he's got it all: he's tall, he's dark, he's handsome. Kind of treats me nicely. It's a bit of a turn-on – he's above me in that he's my editor, that kind of relationship. I like it.

I was finding something quite interesting in that my hips go out but then my knees go in and I feel like I've got like love handles. I wanted to see how other naked women look so yesterday I typed *naked women* in Google. I find naked women more attractive than naked men; I just think we're more attractive. I clicked on this picture and it took me to porn and I was thinking, actually I'm not turned on by porn. I'm turned on by naked women more than by porn. Yeah. I didn't know that about myself. With porn if I have my vibrator I can do whatever but I never feel that good after. I get high and I really sink low. I pay attention for a bit, and then I get this low because the women are being degraded; it's not natural, it's all artificial. The man's normally dominant. Quite rough as well sometimes. I think there's still a lot of male domination.

Even though there's been a sexual revolution, I just feel this is a man's world. We've put out that women are freer than ever, but I don't think we quite are. Back in the summer there was this trend with hot denim shorts where you can literally see the bum cheeks hanging out; is it for the validation of men? Are we objects more than ever? I think for our generation, the word that comes to mind is 'rough'; everything is going to be more rough for us.

Having Indian parents and being English does affect your sexuality. Sex isn't really talked about. I remember my mum, when I was eleven years old, she was like, 'Do you want me to teach you about the birds and the bees?' My mum was really easygoing like that. I went, 'No, Mum, I feel a bit awkward.' My mum really didn't want to marry my dad; her father forced her to. She was twenty-one. She even tried to commit suicide. Her father actually beat her up. He was a headmaster in India and the family had high status because of that. My dad's side were village people. Really odd pairing of my mum and dad.

If I introduced a guy to my dad and he's white, my dad could take it. Black, no. Muslim, no. Those two we just can't go for. I don't have a fantasy about black guys. I wouldn't be open to marrying a Muslim guy. I would only have a fantasy about someone I could probably marry. I'd go along with an arranged marriage. If the guy's nice. But I'd really want to get to know the guy, I wouldn't just go, 'Okay, in a couple of months we're getting married.' One or two years and then we'll see. I wouldn't pretend to be a virgin. No. If he's from this country I don't think he'd be innocent. When I go into my marriage I'm not going to pretend to be someone I'm not. I'm going to be straight with him, so he knows what he's dealing with. Maybe in the future I'll find someone but right now it's not happening, maybe I've got too much baggage, maybe I've got to sort out my values.

To be honest my dad hasn't got time to arrange a marriage. He married another woman quite quickly – one year after my mum died. He went to India, he saw this woman and he married her. Then she came here but it didn't work out and so he's going through a divorce. A couple of months ago my dad was talking to this woman from Birmingham; I think he was thinking of marrying again. My sister said to my dad, 'You're fifty years old, don't you think you should be trying to find me a husband?' He goes, 'Well, I've got my own life to lead.' So it doesn't look like we're going to be getting an arranged marriage.

Because I haven't had sex for a long time, what's been in my brain is having lots of casual sex, no-strings-attached sex. That's what I want now. But I'm two-minded about it. Number one, I don't want to get attached like I've done in the past and, number two, where to find it? Fantasy's not satisfying any more. It's got to the point where I just want a casual one-night fling. I was trying to find what the best phone app is if you want casual sex with someone and my friend goes, '*Blendrr* is a good one.' And I'll be honest, I've got like fifty messages from guys: the thing is, they're not good-looking! There was this guy, he was a bit older but he was all right looking but he kind of put me off. He goes, 'Do you want me to come over?' 'Actually I live with my dad and my sister.' He said, 'Maybe a hotel room?' I stopped talking to him. The ugly ones I just delete. There's this really good-looking guy, he doesn't really reply, he doesn't talk that much: good-looking guys are like that, I think.

I just. Want. Good. Old. Sex. Like it was when I was fifteen – the first time I had sex. That's what I want: the orgasms. I only had sex with Marvin, the first guy, once but it really worked. He wasn't that good-looking. I was horny so I contacted

Marvin recently and we were texting and I was really turning him on with these messages, I was going: 'I'm messaging you naked.' I was making him go mad. Something stopped me going through with it; I don't know what it was. Marvin was going to come over twice. I backed away. He goes, 'We should have done it more.' I might as well do it now while I'm young. I don't want to do it in three years' time when I'm married and he's married. And then there's the personal trainer from the gym – Adrian. Oh God! Very – again – good-looking and handsome. When he was giving me a free personal training session I touched his arm, which was really muscly. I don't know what it was; it was like an orgasm. It just felt so good when I touched him. That's when I started to kind of think, 'Do I look fit?' Only I want to lose weight before sex, I don't want him to think, 'She's got a flabby belly.' I might get working on it.'

# 10

# Face

Deborah, 41, Leicester

*'I'm attracted to horrible men'*

'If I was being honest about my sexual fantasy, I could say things like 'I'd love to have sex in a walk-in shower,' for example. Don't know why. But I would. I like men in pink shirts! I swing between fantasising about a therapist who used to look after me years ago, about him having sex with me really gently, but then I also have a bigger thing about wanting to be raped again. In actual fact, the rape fantasy is far bigger for me but in both those fantasies I'm never turned on. Sometimes I try and think sexually when I watch *The Bodyguard* with Kevin Costner. I don't get sexually aroused but I get really emotionally aroused which I'm aware for a woman can be quite closely related. I don't want to have sex with Kevin Costner but I do want him to look after me, to protect me. There's that bit where he lifts her up in his arms it's like, 'Oh Kevin. Do that to me.'

But when people ask me about sex, this is what I say: 'I haven't had sex since 1993, and if I never have it again, I will be a very happy woman.' And as far as I'm aware I've never had an orgasm. I think I'd know if I'd had one! If it's as good as they say, I think I would have remembered! I haven't kissed a man since 1999. Do I think my life is any less for it? No. Actually I think my life is a lot simpler without men and without sex, to be frank.

But then I had a very recent incident. I'm attracted to horrible men; I just find horrible men more attractive than nice men. I had this man come to the door trying to sell me dusters and cleaning stuff; he was obviously a complete charlatan and he tried to come on to me and I actually *physically* felt attracted to him. And I don't think I've ever felt that; it was so weird. It was like: if I didn't think my lodger was going to come home I would have just had him on the floor. It was such a new experience. It was like – what on *earth* was that?

What attracted me to the salesman was he was a bit of a git: that was part of the problem. He was young. He did have quite nice pecs! But he was obviously a complete charlatan. He'd told me he'd been in prison and he told me what for: grievous bodily harm. So, of course, immediately there's this thing that triggers off in me: a violent man. I have a pull towards them. And he was being very suggestive, to say the least. He was asking me what kind of massage I liked and he actually asked me for a kiss. When I told some friends they were mortified and shocked because I could *easily* have had sex with a random stranger.

One thing that has really affected my sexual identity is I was born with a really rare condition. There are two forms of it, one is the genetic form, which I don't have: I'm just a complete freak; the odds are millions. Before I was born my brain grew too big so my skull wasn't joined which meant that the whole centre part of my face was misaligned and I was born without a nose and with eyes displaced to the side of my face. The first lot of surgery was not until I was eleven. That meant I spent the whole of primary school looking very odd. The surgeon used a material like Plasticine to build a nose and, to me, it looked so awful that when I walked past somebody I would pretend I had an itch and I would scratch the top of my nose but I did that so obsessively I actually wore away the Plasticine.

Children are cruel so I had, right from the word go, people being horrible about my face. I was taunted as 'ET' as a teenager, and 'flat face'. I remember when I was going on the bus to secondary school there was this really pervy bus driver and he said, 'How are you?' and I said, 'Oh, I'm all the better for seeing you.' Some children at the back of the bus said, 'She's got to say that because she ain't going to get nobody else, that's the best she's going to get.' That kind of stuff really stayed with me. That's part of why my dad could do what he did because there was this sense that I would never get anyone else and someone was better than no one.

The reality is I'm forty-one and I still get lots of comments about my face, which have left me a complete wreck. I have people to this day shout out across the street how ugly I am, and recently when I was on breakfast telly talking about doing jigsaw puzzles, somebody put the clip on YouTube and this person wrote the most awful comment under the YouTube video: there was an alien I looked like. I got some of the comments taken off; I don't know if there are any more. I don't look now. I just can't bear it. I remember once when I lived in Leicester I was walking through a churchyard and this bloke came up to me – I'd never met him before – and said, 'You're so fucking ugly,' and walked off! That's what he said to me. I was like, 'Oh, why would you do that?'

How I look has been a *massive* thing for me, and for men. I will speak to friends and they will all say I'm lovely and I look nice, but in reality I have random people being horrible about my face. Then I get really confused because I know some real mingers and they've got married, and I think, well, what's *that* about? They're having sex. So I know there's something more to it than what we look like. Sometimes I look at people and think, 'Oh, surely I'm not as ugly as you?' Which is such a terribly judgmental thing to say. I have spent my whole life at the hands of people who have made my life hell because of the way I look, but I am aware that I am as judgmental with other people. I am completely aware of that to my shame, it's not something I'm proud of.

When I go into primary schools to teach, the children tend to look at me at first but once I've opened my mouth and they've met my personality it's not an issue, and part of the reason I've got quite a vivacious personality is overcompensation. But if I'm in a pub or a disco and a man comes up to me I automatically think they are taking the piss and doing it for a bet to see if they can pull the ugliest bitch in the room. I'm so self-conscious about how I look and if I was being brutally honest I think I'm so ugly that no man would ever want to kiss me or hold my gaze. And the blokes that had sex with me very rarely kissed me because kissing is the most intimate thing you can do. The salesman, the infamous salesman, was trying to chat me up because he wanted me to buy stuff off him; I had no illusion. He actually took my number – stupidly I gave it to him – and, of course, I never heard from him and I didn't think that I would but ... yeah. Dirty old men find me attractive. Married men that want a shag find me attractive, but nice single guys who aren't going to hurt me don't find me attractive, which is a bit of a bummer, really.

I didn't grow up in a Christian home – not at all. There was no Christian influence – quite the opposite – and it was a horrible, overtly sexual environment. I always went with my parents to the pub and when I was twelve my mum got Dad a stripogram for his birthday and I was taking pictures of my dad with this stripogram. I look back now, as a teacher, and I wouldn't be very happy if one of my Year 7s told that to me.

I had a very complicated, incestuous relationship with my dad. My mum was in hospital for over a year and at that time I was sleeping with him and I became his wife; it was a bit like the Stockholm syndrome, I was utterly in love with my dad. I have to say it was a very confused time for me. I think it was when I was about thirteen or fourteen, for just over a year, and it didn't go on afterwards because my mum came back. And I hated my mum with a vengeance for coming back, absolutely hated her. She's dead as well. Absolutely hated her because she took him away from me.

My mum handled everything so badly. For example, I have always struggled – and I think this is mostly linked with not wanting sex – with washing, with keeping myself clean. I'm a lot better than I've ever been and, unless I'm depressed, I will religiously shower every other day; that's the most I can get to. I work very hard at having a shower every other day, I tell you, but it's bloody hard work sometimes. As a teenager I didn't wash at all and some of that was I felt so dirty on the inside that I wanted a physical mark on the outside to show that I was dirty. Some of it was I couldn't *bear* taking my clothes off and touching my own body. Some of it was that at home there was never a lock on the bathroom door. Having a bath was not safe for me. I remember when I started my periods, which was a real awful awfulness to me, and I'd got blood on my knickers and my mum showing my dad my soiled knickers saying, 'Look what your daughter's done.' I just remember dying a million deaths.

Since my dad's died – he's been dead eight years – I'm stuck in that grief of him. When my dad died, to all intents and purposes I probably died with him. I've often said, 'I might just as well have got in the coffin with him,' because I think when we have sex with somebody, that soul tie, that bond, that yoke, whatever terminology we use, is so powerful and when it's used negatively in the sense of a control mechanism it's very hard to break. I'm currently stuck in that process of not being able to let him go. I would give anything to have him back. Would I sleep with him again? As an adult? I'd really like to think not but ... He was a bastard but I was in love with him, you know. In the wrong sense. Completely in the wrong sense. But he's gone, and I wish he hadn't gone, I wish he was still here even though he was horrible to me. It was a complete idolisation, a wrong kind of love. It felt like being taken over and I felt I couldn't live. So Dad was just really, really complicated.

When I was a teenager my dad was on the scene so I never had a normal boyfriend. I was enmeshed with my dad, really. I didn't want anyone else. Since my twenties, I've had the gits who just want sex. Yep. In terms of the very negative sexual experiences I've had, that has been because bullies can sniff out victims – definitely. I give off a sense of, 'You can do what you want to me because I won't say no to you.' I think predators sniff out their prey. Two of the men were vicars. They were both married and they were both my priests at the time. With one of the priests – I was in a psychiatric hospital and I was let out into his care and he slept with me that night. Then I had an affair with a guy who was very like my dad – that wasn't great. My experience up to my fiancé has been shagging married men. I was always the other woman in real life. Yep. Always the other woman. Obviously this is twenty years ago I'm talking about. What it's done is left me with this legacy of, 'I'm quite a good-time girl, I'm quite a good sexual partner, I'll do whatever men want ultimately.' But they can always say goodbye; they can always leave me. They don't have to put up with me. They can get what they want but then they're not the ones that are having to deal with me if I've got a headache. After having sex, these blokes usually wanted to have sex again; what I wanted was for them to stay in bed with their arm around me. They wouldn't, obviously. Or they wanted to get up and go because they could. I've never had an experience of sex equating with love. Do I think a man can love me without having sex with me? No. In my mind, if I want a man then I've got to be willing to do what the man wants. Well, actually I hope I'm not sick, but oral sex and swallowing the sperm I find *really* horrendous, but they want that, so because they want it, I do it. Oh gosh, I think I'm going to be sick ... I won't be sick. Oh. Phew ...

When I became a Christian, sex outside of marriage was bad. So the things that I did with my fiancé weren't full intercourse, but to all intents and purposes it was a sexual relationship, just with guilt invested. The guilt was awful. The actual acts were pretty awful. He enjoyed them. There was no enjoyment for me but a lot of guilt. Whereas with that salesman it was like, do you know what, if I'd have had sex with him I might have enjoyed it. Possibly. How outrageous would that have been? I don't think I could have coped with the guilt. Partly I wouldn't have coped with the guilt of not being married but I would have felt *absolutely mortified* at me enjoying sex. Because I shouldn't, basically. Enjoying something that was sin – to use the Christian term – would have been horrendous for me. Sex therapists would have a field day with me with this: if I enjoy something, why does a part of me feel like I'm betraying some painful part of me?

So the last time I had sex was in 1993. What I did with my fiancé – who was a git and he didn't marry me, he married somebody else – was that for six years my life became centred round him and I wouldn't do things so I could see him. And I know that's what I used to do with my dad, it started there, I would sacrifice stuff if I could go out with Dad. Because my dad – unfortunately – helped foster in me a sense of 'I can't be alive by myself,' that to survive I needed him, and that started at a very young age. I'm so weak around men emotionally that if I was to get involved with one I'd be swallowed up. I don't want that. I'd rather be alone than that. That is the worst feeling, waiting for that phone to go or for a text: I'm not doing that for all the tea in China.

I'm glad I don't have sex but I have moments of fear that I'm going to be an old bitter spinster, which I don't like. I obviously don't let myself think this very often but I do have this moment of thinking I'd love to be married, and what I'd love more than anything is for someone to sit on the sofa watching telly with me, that there'd be somebody when I come home from work; that I'm not always coming into an empty house. But I do not want random sexual encounters because I don't want to have to wash my sheets! I'd like someone on the sofa – as long as they don't make a mark! The shower is better because at least it will all rub off. I'll have to wear ear muffs so I don't hear anything. And I'd have to be blindfolded so I can't see them looking at me. It's not looking great really, is it? I do sometimes think it would be good to have sex in a walk-in shower, but then when I try and think about having sex in a walk-in shower there's absolutely nothing, it's just like, no. Then I think, well, actually the fantasy doesn't give me any enjoyment in the slightest so I don't bother having the fantasy. I'm all right with my jigsaw puzzles, really!

There's an asexuals' group; I heard about it on Radio 4 – I love Radio 4 – but then some friends were like, 'Deborah – you are *not* asexual.' But is asexual different to being celibate? Celibate is a choice; asexuals don't have a choice. Even when I think of Simon Cowell who is the typical bad boy with a horrible persona, the kind of guy I'd be attracted to, the thought of sex with him doesn't do it for me. You know, I can live a fuller life as far as my understanding of a full life is without having sex; sex is not going to make any difference. My therapist's challenge to me when I spoke to her last week was, 'Deborah – I believe you can have that part of life as much as anybody else can have it.' I don't. But am I sitting here thinking, 'Oh gosh, I've missed out because I'm not having sex?' No. Quite relieved, in fact!'

# 11

# Healer

Gwyn, 49, London

*'Pleasure is a great healer'*

'My partner will come home from work and say, 'I taught this kid how to play the piano,' and I'm like, 'I did a fanny massage!' He says, 'Oh, yeah, you have a different job from me!' I'm like, 'Yeah, pretty much!' Probably I have an unusual job, I can't remember, I'm so immersed in a world where it's normal. For the last ten years I've been helping people work with their sexuality, to heal it, or change it, or open it up and discover more about themselves as sexual beings.

Vaginal massage is beautiful. Some people call it 'yoni massage'. Some people say 'vulva massage'. 'Cunt massage', actually, some people. Lots of women don't have their genitals focused on unless someone wants something from them. Somebody's only gone there to wipe them, to give them a gynaecological exam or because they want pleasure but never to just say, 'Well, what you got going on here? Let's have a look. Oh, what's your clitoris do?' To give it attention and to say, 'Why, you're beautiful, let's honour you.'

Vaginal massage is always a great honour and it's always a very beautiful thing to do. I do it for different reasons. For some women it's because something hurts there or isn't quite working and they want healing. Sometimes they want to find their pleasure again. A recent massage was for a woman who was married for a long time, she had said no to sex early on, raised the kids, and she'd suddenly had a spontaneous sexual awakening, wanted to find out more about herself and didn't want to do it with her husband. She said, 'I'd like you to help me figure out what's going on around there.' So we did it like a fun adventure and exploration.

I always ask permission for each move I make. I start with lots of massage on the body, then focus on opening the hips and the thighs and getting them relaxed and then I eventually do some stuff on the outside of the vagina, just holding, and massaging around the public bone and the bum and the inner thighs because it's all connected. Also, for a woman to let you in she has to feel relaxed and safe. I am taking the outer labia and pressing it and rolling it. Some women want it done quite hard, some women don't. We hold tension in our genitals – well, women who come here do – so it's about relaxing the muscles and the skin and the fibres, giving it love, telling it it's beautiful. Sometimes women are holding their thoughts in there, their fear, shame.

I always start on the outside, lots of stroking, lots of calming. Some women might say, 'Carry on,' or they might say, 'I need a break,' or it will bring stuff up and they're in floods of tears. Eventually if it feels right I'll say, 'Can I enter?' I might go inside the lips first and a little bit on the clitoral button without actually penetrating, *then* ask about penetration. I start with one finger with the pad up and to really slowly, slowly, slowly, slowly let her body take you in and then be still and let her get used to that ... and then I might press. The idea is to release tension inside. We map the clitoris out like a clock. Then very slowly when we both feel ready I'd move to one o'clock, two o'clock, three o'clock ... First of all I might use pressure and they might say, 'Can you do little circles?' or, 'Can you tap?' or, 'Can you press harder?' so we see what the clitoris wants and we move and we keep moving.

Sometimes they orgasm. With some women it's the first time they've felt arousal in a long time. Some of them are going, 'Oh, oh, I'm all turned on,' and I'm like, 'Great! Do you want to run with that?' And they might say, 'Oh, is that allowed? I don't know, oh, but it feels so good.' 'It's up to you.' Pleasure is a great healer.

I had one client who couldn't orgasm. She wanted, at her request, to masturbate in front of me, so as she got close to orgasming I could tell her what to do to get her over the edge. I was watching her and she was orgasming. She wasn't having a big expression but her body was doing it all. I said to her, 'That's an orgasm.' She said, 'What do you mean?' I said. 'It's not the big be-all-and-end-all, but it is orgasmic energy.' And she was like, 'It is?' I was like, 'If you can learn to ride that wave you'll get to the bigger ones.' She emailed me weeks later and said, 'Oh my God, I can orgasm now!' So for her it was me witnessing what was going on and her tweaking it a little bit.

My background wasn't open but it wasn't massively shameful either. Normalish, I guess. I remember at thirteen finding my dad's *Playboy* magazines and it felt like coming home. It was like, 'Wow, beautiful. Naked bodies!' and I was most interested in the sex stories. I remember feeling very excited – what I know now is turned on – and a little bit of shame because the magazines had been hidden and I knew not to tell anyone I was looking at them. But there was something very familiar and safe to me in them. There was always a big draw to sex and it always felt good and normal and exciting to me. As I went through my life I had lots of good experiences but I had a lot of bad experiences as well, sexually. And everything in between. Lots of different relationships, marriages, the whole thing.

Before this, I was doing massage in a charity for people with disabilities. When I went on the training course to do this work, I could not say the word 'cunt'. When I grew up it was the worst word that you could ever say, worse than 'fuck', worse than 'bitch'. In fact, I would have struggled to say 'the c word' even, because that referred to *cunt*! Couldn't do it. The first week of the training course, I was absolutely terrified. One woman on the course looked round at the men and says, 'I'd like to sing you a song I've written. It's called "The Cunt Song".' And she sings this gorgeous song set to this jazzy tune about, 'Oh, piss, flap, cunt, vagina ...' And all these crass terms for vagina and vulva and the chorus was, 'It's the holiest holy hole'.

She said we need to reclaim the word 'cunt'. It's used in a derogatory way – so: 'you cunt!' Why would we say that about our most sacred place? We do it with 'dick' as well: 'He's a dick.' 'She's a cunt.' We used our genitals as swear words because they're shameful. I started practising saying the word 'cunt'. I wanted to be an empowered woman! I wanted to claim mine back. Roll forward many years and I ran a workshop called Cunt Love. We started with, 'What do you call yours?' Nobody would speak so we wrote down all the words we could think of for vulva and vagina and put them up in the room and tried to get women to say them, and they couldn't. What *is* it when we can't say the name of our bodies? I couldn't even say 'cock' too! Instead of 'penis'. Now I say it all the time. I love it. Great word!

In another training workshop, we were in groups with four women. We showed our cunt and talked about it and said, 'This is what it looks like, I quite like this bit,' and, 'I shave mine because ...' or, 'I don't shave mine because ...'. 'I like it when ...' and, 'These are some good times we've had together and these are some bad times,' and talked about it while they looked at it. It was one of the most amazing things I ever did. It was the first time in my life I realised, 'Oh yeah, yours is different from mine! Cool!' It's quite hard to see the vagina – it's not like the penis. Definitely not like the penis.

Sometimes the women I work with go on to have more fulfilled sex lives. A lot of women learn to masturbate better, because a lot of them don't masturbate, or not much, or not well. They know, 'Touch this part of the clitoris and not that part,' or, 'I need to use a dildo,' or, 'I don't need to use a dildo,' or whatever it is. They learn more about their own bodies and what works so that they have better orgasms, whether that's on their own or with a partner. Mostly, though, I work with men.

Men come to see me for lots of different reasons. Things like premature ejaculation or difficulty getting or maintaining an erection. I see men who have little or no experience of sexuality. There was a chap today and I'm the only person he's had any sexual experience with. He's thirty-seven. A virgin. Right as he hit puberty he needed some operations. He then decided his body was disgusting, horrible and disfigured, and he shut down. A little bit of body dysmorphia going on there. He thinks his body's grotesque; there's a scar here or there. I keep showing him my scars, I go, 'Look! People have scars.' He has very low self-esteem. It's been twenty years of him dealing with that and he's terrified of being with a woman and not knowing what to do and getting it wrong and of her rejecting him because of his body.

I work with men who can't orgasm – or don't orgasm – often because there's a fear of release. They were told early on, '*Don't* you get a woman pregnant!' A lot of men are frightened of being powerful, or fear letting go. Many men want to learn to separate orgasm from ejaculation. Because for men orgasm is separate from ejaculation – well, for women also, but that's a whole other thing. So orgasms are all nice feelings, ripples through the body, while ejaculation is the expulsion of semen. It happens at the same time unless you learn to separate it or you're very lucky. They want to orgasm without ejaculating to last longer. They want to have sex for longer.

Some men come because they want to learn to be a better lover. I used to get a lot of emails where guys would say, 'I want to learn methods and techniques for pleasing a woman.' I would teach them how to touch a woman to a degree. But I would always say, 'You don't need to learn methods and techniques. Maybe a few – touch this bit and not that, and make sure there's enough lubricant.' But it's not about techniques. Most of what I teach is how to be present. Because if you can be present with someone, you will intuitively know what to do.

One chap came here and he wanted to figure out how to please his wife, he didn't think he was pleasing her very well and part of that was he really had a bit of an obsession with breasts and he would keep playing with her breasts when she asked him to stop. He said, 'She'll ask me to stop but I can't, I'm really focused on them.' So I said, 'Well, that's not going to be pleasing her! Imagine I was playing with your penis and you asked me to stop and I kept playing with it?' and he was like, '*Oh!*' Finally struck home.

We did this session and I could *feel* as if his inner baby was *desperate* for breasts, *starved*. Like a bit of him was almost withered and desiccated. I said, 'This is what I feel, and I think this is why you struggle to let go of your wife's breasts when you get access to them.' He was like, 'Yeah ...' That made sense to him. We agreed it would feel good for him to receive that mothering energy he needed. Held him like a baby and, oh! it was fascinating because the way he held my breast and put his mouth there and sucked was just like my daughter used to. It was baby, it was not man. After a few sucks he went into bliss and peace, calmed right down, and I don't know how long we were like that. Then I moved him over to the other side. One gets sore! Afterwards he was blissed out. He emailed me a while ago: his whole life's changed, everything looks different, he feels more grounded, he's much more present with his wife.

I've seen musicians and lawyers and people in the church, people from all religions, Muslim, Jewish, Christian. The majority of the male clients are Caucasian. A lot are Indian, Asians. Far fewer black men. All different financial backgrounds, lots of businessmen, some hippified people, artists, lots of engineers, and bankers. Anybody! Anybody! Sessions are a minimum of two hours. And it goes really quickly. We have a chat, we decide together what we're going to do. Usually we move to a mat on the floor. Often I'm naked or clients are naked. I'm trying to get someone to relax, become present in their body and limbering up arousal. For some people just gentle strokes on their body and they're in tears, or angry, or back into memories. For others, being allowed to experience pleasure and not be rejected for it is healing. It's like, oh it *is* okay for me to experience pleasure. For some people it means being witnessed in their arousal and not being judged and still being loved.

They don't have to pull me or emotionally tangle with me, they don't have to do my washing-up. Men rarely get attached to me. I would say that I'm *so* clear with what I'm offering, and I'm *so* clear with boundaries. I mean, I get a few adoring fans but they're not attached in any unhealthy way. I never feel scared. I've always trusted my intuition, one thousand per cent. I trust my own instinct and I've never been wrong. When I was first doing this work a friend said I should have a rape alarm, so I had one for a few years. Forgot all about it, found it a few years ago, I was like, 'I don't need this any more; I'm not afraid to take anyone where they need to go any more.' So I chucked that out. No, I don't feel afraid.

The youngest I've worked with is twenty-one, which was pretty much on the edge for me. The oldest was eighty. He told me all sorts of sexual desires he'd had in his life but they had been shamed out of him through boys' public school. He had shut off his sexual self. He got to a point where he was like, 'Screw that. I'm not getting any younger. I want this part of me back! And I want to be touched!' He hadn't been touched in fifteen years.

So many people I see never get hugged. They live on their own or with a flatmate and they work in an office and they come home again. People don't hug out there in the world. It's painful. Painful. A few months ago I started something called Cuddle Sessions. No sexual touch. Both of us dressed or in pyjamas and just holding, and a lot of people came for it. But even in sessions where there's something much more sexual-looking going on, it always ends with a deep holding. People need to know that their bodies are acceptable and that their desires are acceptable and it's okay to be held.

I come across a lack of sex education. Most parents don't talk about sex. And mainstream porn is not doing anyone favours. I had one man come to me, he was thirty-two, he'd never had sex because he told me that his penis was deformed and disfigured. He was really upset by this. We emailed a lot – he was too afraid to come for a session. After a *year* of emailing, I said, 'Look, don't come for a session; come for a cup of tea. Come for a chat.' I thought, what is going on? I was googling all these different disfigurations of the penis. Eventually he came and I said, 'I'm going to have to take a look, because I'm not going to be able to help you unless I know what I'm dealing with.' And he'd never been naked in front of a woman. I get that a lot.

Eventually he managed to take down his trousers, take down his underpants, and I see this *beautiful* penis hanging there. He was like, 'Please tell me if I'll ever be able to have sex.' I was like, 'What do you think is wrong with it?' He said, 'It hangs to the left. I've seen porn and I know that they hang straight and mine doesn't hang straight.' I said to him, 'Most men hang to one side or the other; you never see a flaccid penis in porn, so you wouldn't know. When you're erect you're straight?' He was like, 'Yeah, I am.' I was like, 'So it's the same.'

I said, 'Even if your penis wasn't normal because it hung to the left, women's vaginas *stretch*. Babies can come out of there!' He thought because it hung slightly to the left that he would hurt a woman. He had a few sessions and got to the point where he accepted that he was normal. What he really needed to do was just put his penis in a woman's vagina to see that it would fit. Which is not something I offer. I referred him to a colleague who would do that and again another year went by – he was too afraid to do it. Eventually out of the blue I got a message from him saying, 'I saw your colleague. She's amazing! You're amazing! I did it! I put it in! I'm normal!' He's free and liberated, he's dating.

Everyone to some degree has some concern around their sexuality. Whatever society, background, religion you grow up in, someone's usually been taught fear, shame and guilt, or they've picked it up from society or advertising. Most people have travelled up to their head and they value thinking and intellect, and very few people live embodied. I think everyone is suffering sexually. Some people figure it out and have great sex lives. I just don't see them that often. I've seen people who were married for twenty-something years and they've got divorced and there was no sex for the last ten years. Or people who are still married however many years down the line but there is no communication between them and they've suppressed who they were. Or their desires were rejected early on. I saw a man who was married for forty years but for thirty-nine of those years they'd slept in separate rooms at her request. He said, 'I love her, I don't want to leave her but I'm missing a huge chunk of who I am.' He said, 'I don't want to go and see an escort but I need someone to wake my body up, remind me who I am as a sexual being.' He had it back for himself. Which for me is the most important thing.

I get turned on. Yeah. Often. *Yeah*! With both men and women. I'm using my sexual energy to draw their sexual energy out, not in a 'Come on, baby, let's do it' way. It's more like, my sexual energy is always on to some degree or another but I use it as a kind of like a template for their energy to come. I meet them where they are and then I turn it up a degree. There might be the desire in my body to have sex with them, the awareness that it would feel really good to have something penetrate me, but I don't do that, because the sessions are not about my pleasure. I'm very clear that my needs and pleasures are taken care of outside of a session. I use my sexual energy to help this person who's come to me expand and explore their sexuality, like a teacher might use their intelligence to create intelligence but they are probably going somewhere else to get their intellectual needs met. There might be the desire for penetration but it's never that 'Oh, God! I have to have it now!' It's more like, I can say to somebody, 'Can you see and feel my body is turned on and aroused, this is you doing it,' and they're, 'Oh, wow! I can turn someone on! Hurray!'

Up until last week it would be *absolutely no* penetrative sex ever for anyone. Most of the time whatever it is someone needs from me does not require penetration. Just doesn't. I want to get someone to the point where they're ready and confident and can go out and create their own sex life. They don't need to get that need met with me. But last week, my partner said, 'I feel like our relationship is evolving and your work is evolving, and were you to feel it was necessary for someone's highest good it would be okay.' I said, 'Wow, that's new.' I started thinking about, have I ever needed to do that? Honestly, in the ten years I've been doing it, I'd say there were ten people where I thought that's what they needed from me. And in those cases, it wasn't gratuitous, although I hesitate to use 'gratuitous' around pleasure, because what's gratuitous pleasure? But one of them just needed to put it in to see if it was possible.

I'm so blessed to be with my partner. He's actually gender-queer but he's a man. Most of the time. He was born into a male body. He told me that he always wanted to be with someone who was in the sex industry, because he felt sex was so important that it rules everyone's lives in some way, whether they're getting it or not. Written in the stars or what? Every time my partner and I have penetrative sex I find myself going, 'Oh my God, it's still happening!' because in all my other relationships sex fell off after ten, twenty times. I still wanted it, but they didn't. Every time my partner's inside me it's like, 'Wow, you still want to be inside me!' Seven and a half years later, that's still being desired of me. I am sexually satisfied. Yeah! With my partner, it deepens all the time. And because we both – this might sound weird – we can both move in and out of gender. Sometimes he's the woman and I'm the man, he's more gender-fluid than I am. And we play with power play as well, sometimes one of us is dominant, the other submissive. Sometimes we shape-shift and become other beings beside human.

We talk of our sex lives in terms of Thorpe Park – the amusement park. We say, there's the rides we know well and we go on frequently because they're right at the beginning of the park and it's easy. Then there's some other rides, they're a bit further back: when we've got time we go visit those rides. And there are some rides we know we'd like to go on sometime but the time has to be right. And there are whole parts of the park that aren't even built yet, and that's really exciting. And other parts are still under construction. So we can never get bored. We've got all these realms to play in and it never gets boring.'

## 12

# Feminist

Shirley, seventies, Leeds

*'There was always somebody ready to come and have sex with me'*

'When I was sixteen I met my first husband. I went to this party, I met him, that was it, I was totally in love with him from that minute on. Arthur was at university. For me, oh God! that was exciting. I knew I could never get to university. Nobody in my family had ever gone – I came from a very working-class family. It was one of those fantastic things that other people did, like people went on holiday abroad. It's incredible to think how different life was then.

The first date we had he told me his father had died that day, so instead of going to the cinema we went for a walk. I first had sex with him – and when I think back, oh my God! I wouldn't do that now – when his mother was in the house. My God, it was so risky. This was before we were married; I was sixteen, Arthur was nineteen. I was scared because it was not the right thing to do: it was against my morality – I knew that. But I was also very keen to have sex. I was a sexy girl. I was always desperate for it.

I think because I was adopted – I'm sure this happens in ordinary families but this is my view of it – I didn't fit my parents. They got landed with me, which must have been the shock of their lives. They had got this beautiful baby at six weeks and I turned into a really wild child. And they didn't know what to do with me. I'd be outside cuddling a boyfriend, I would be out late, my dad would come looking for me because he was frightened that anything could happen to me: 'Come on, lady! Or else.' I don't think people do this now. It was crazy! My dad would come out and he'd go one way and we ran the other way and then I'd be back home before him. I'm so ashamed now when I think of it. But I think it's the strength of one's sexual feelings, really.

When I was eighteen I went to be a nurse in Sheffield. In those days there were matrons and it was all very strict. God knows what made me think I could be a nurse. I remember the first time I went on the wards I fainted, I was never going to be a nurse. Never. But the idea was to get away from home; it didn't matter what I did. Arthur came to Sheffield to a chemical company on his university placement and he had a little flat. Then of course the inevitable happened and I got pregnant and I didn't tell anybody. I didn't tell a soul. I knew I was going to have to tell people I was pregnant and the whole world was going to be mad with me.

I told my mum and dad; they were horrified. They were furious at Arthur. Oh my God, it was awful. My family were difficult; they said Arthur was too thin. Arthur's family thought I wasn't good enough for him because they were an academic family. They lived in a little house – a very poor house because the money had all been spent on sending the four boys to university. Where I lived wasn't rough but it was a village outside the town and they thought, 'This little ...!' I was very insensitive to them. I thought I was okay, but looking back, I think, 'Oh, Shirley!' I was like my granddaughters are with me now: 'I know everything! You know nothing!' So a bit of that. It was decided – there was no thought about it – that we were going to get married. My mum and dad said they would buy me a wedding dress because they wanted it to look as if it was a real wedding. And it all happened and we got married in church. His family refused to come, which is interesting in itself.

We stayed with my mum and dad, then I had Richard. Arthur graduated and eventually we could afford to buy a house in Leeds because they were cheap. Then my mum was making noises about, 'Are you going to have another child?' This was in the sixties. Arthur was not interested in sex. He had a very low sex drive and I didn't. I remember one time he came home and I said, 'Come here.' 'No.' I realise looking back: that is weird when you're twenty-one. Once we went to stay the night at his boss's house – him and his wife were charming – and Arthur wouldn't have sex because he didn't want to mess the sheets. By that time, or very shortly after that, I had affairs with people, one affair after another. I was having affair after affair. I'd be nineteen, twenty. I was obviously really needy.

I was like a little Stepford wife. Arthur would invite his bridge group over – I was making stuffed tomatoes for them. I was the little one at home with the boys. I was having sex with my husband but not very satisfactorily at all. We had a lovely 1930s house in Leeds, a front room with a bay window, and a dining room with doors out to the garden and a lovely breakfast room – it was a lovely, lovely house. I was very happy with my two boys, and I had this sex on the side, always, and when one person went, another person just appeared. I remember thinking, 'This is like a sort of magic.' Somebody went, there was always somebody else waiting in the wings. It was almost as if there was nobody that I wouldn't have sex with. I think they were all married. Sometimes it was friends' husbands. I think I was starving, actually, sexually. I lived quite happily with my husband at the same time as having affairs with people I met at the library and, interestingly, mostly men from other cultures: Asian men, African men. Other cultures meant excitement, exotic, interest, something different, with lots to learn about the culture, about everything. Exciting. I always did want to do exciting things and be with exciting men. I've always been involved with foreign men, always.

Eventually I thought, 'I can't do this my whole life long.' I told Arthur I'd had all these affairs – maybe thirty, something like that, a lot. He went into shock. I said, 'How could you not know?' Because he did things like bring his friends home – young men from work – and they'd sit around. He'd go to bed and leave me with them. When I look back I think, 'That's not normal.' Now, with my ability to think psychoanalytically, I think something was going on! I always thought I was a very bad person. But was I? Was I really the baddie? It wasn't as if I was immoral, but it looks as if I was. So interesting.

I went to some event at the City Hall and met this penniless Mexican seven years younger than me – I was twenty-six, he was nineteen – and just totally fell in love, whatever that is. And had sex all the time at the beginning. Terrific. I ran off with Javier to a bedsit in Hastings and I left my children and, oh God, it was a terrible time in my life. I was happy in a way but I missed my children very much. I cried several times to come back to my husband. I wanted to come back and I wanted it to be okay but I just couldn't. I'd come back for a day and it was as if I'd died, then I would go to this other guy again. And eventually Arthur said he was divorcing me.

Because I was so afraid that Arthur would commit suicide, when we got divorced I left Richard with Arthur; that was another terrible mistake I made. I think Richard's never forgiven me. And of course Arthur neglected Richard and Richard eventually came to live with me. I made such terrible decisions ... But I was *terrified* Arthur would commit suicide because he was very broken. To tell you the truth, I don't think Arthur ever recovered.

I lived with the two children in this really cheap, ghastly house in Leeds. Did my best with it. Had no money. I was very miserable. The boys and I always used to sleep in the same room because we were scared. I was totally reckless: Javier went to Mexico and I decided I was going to see him. So I left my children with this German lodger I had and I went off to Mexico. I must have been bloody crazy. When we came back, the relationship started to wear off and I got terribly afraid and it all got very ugly. And it's so funny because he got in touch with me latterly – he's a lawyer now – and I thought, 'Oh my God, he is so pompous; what was I doing in those days?' It must have been sex. It was sex, nothing else except sex. Because I think now, 'Oh God Almighty!'

So I came back to Leeds, I went off to university, did my BA in History and English. I remember applying for university and waiting. When I got the letter to say that they'd accepted me I was delirious with joy. It was terrific. Because it opened me up to world literature. I remember reading Solzhenitsyn and going, 'How could I have lived without knowing this?' Terrific. And I did philosophy and all those ideas were fabulous. I graduated and then I got a job in a small school. Oh! In my class I had Muslims, Confucians, I'd have Hindus, people from the Caribbean, I'd have Catholics, I'd have everybody in the same class altogether. It was a wonderful school.

At that time I had a series of boyfriends – I don't know what I must have thought of myself. They were all younger than me. And all very interested in sex, as I was. I had a boyfriend who was a scaffolder but he was a furniture remover as well. I went to York with him in his big furniture van and we – it was crazy – set up the bed. The people were coming the next day and the night before they got there we slept in their bed! There were no curtains so every time I saw a car I thought, '*Oh my God*, they're coming!' I mean, he was totally unsuitable. Then I got somebody else who was equally difficult. That was quite a violent relationship physically. Then there were bits and pieces. There was this other guy and it was sort of finishing but I thought, 'Right, I'll try and revive it. I'm going to Turkey for a month with this man.' So I went to Turkey and I took my two children.

Once we got to Turkey it was obvious this guy wasn't interested. On the third day, I went out with my two little boys on the bus and the bus stopped halfway to Istanbul and everybody got off and this *very* attractive young man came up to me and said, 'Parlez-vous français?' and I said, 'Un petit peu.' Well. That was it! Oh my God. He told me he had been on his way back to university but there had been a military coup and somebody had come into his class and shot someone and the university had been closed, so instead he came swimming with us and we spent the whole week together.

He was Turkish. Another great love affair. I went back and forward to Istanbul the whole time. Eventually in 1979 Amir came here and we got married. We're not married now. We had eleven years together and he is the father of my youngest son, Adam, and, yes, we had some really happy years together.

115

He was fifteen years younger than me, which is a lot. Amir must have been twenty when I met him and I was thirty-five. We were happy together for a while. He was very ... cherishing, I think, is the word. The problem was me, actually. If I'd had some understanding of myself as a person, it would have lasted. I did push him away: it was very difficult for me to make a space for him. When all his books came, I was like, 'Oh, I don't know if I want to make a space for them,' and he had a tiny space for his books.

When I was married to Amir I didn't have affairs, I didn't have to. Because sex was good. I didn't ache to have affairs. I suppose he was my dream man, he was *very* handsome, funny, very hospitable, lovely personality. Maybe that's why I was so devastated when he went. I was devastated, totally devastated, for years. He went off with somebody else whom he's still with – Margaret. I can remember having dreams of tearing Margaret apart with my teeth, because it was so awful. It was the worst time of my life. For years I couldn't see Amir. Adam went to him for weekends but I couldn't see Amir when he came to pick up Adam: I was always not in, or the door was left open.

Two years ago I invited Amir to my birthday and he came. He was delightful. Delightful and delighted. It had been twenty-three years. Then I invited him to stay with us in our house in the Seychelles. And he said to me, 'Yes, but Margaret is coming,' and I met her and I liked her. It was very healing because I realised she was not better than me! But she was very different. He was still very attracted to my way of being because I'm combative: we were very combative. Whereas Margaret will say, 'All right, Amir.' That was never me. I was *never*, 'Okay,' I was always spitting. I've seen them since and I like Margaret very much so that was a very healing experience.

I have wanted to sleep with people since I got divorced but they haven't been around. I haven't slept with anyone for twenty-six years. I remember thinking at the time Amir left, maybe I would never find anyone else but I really didn't believe it, because I was forty-five. I thought I was old but looking back, forty-five is not old. Before, there was always someone in the wings. There was never anybody in the wings after that. Now I'm self-aware to know that wasn't about there not being anyone. It's about me being different. From my twenties there was always somebody ready to come and have sex with me and then there just wasn't. And I wondered what that was about. I was in therapy three times a week for nine years and that changed my life. I have understood why I behaved like that as a girl, as a young woman. I think it was a need for affection.

I've been on my own for so long I've had to look after myself sexually. My sexual fantasies are often historical because I'm very interested in history. It would be in an Elizabethan house. Henry the Eighth would come to the door and he would want sex, and whatever queen it was would go 'Oh my God!' because she was still feeding her child, she was already pregnant; it was too much. She would pass him on to her maid whom, unbeknown to the queen, he'd already had sex with anyway. And the maid was pregnant, everybody was pregnant: there was just no end to this man's need for sex. I've had the fantasy about Henry the Eighth for years and years.

There is another fantasy where the man is really old. And his wife is also very old. They're on a farm in America and she'll be in the barn and he will creep up to her. And take her. From the back. And I'll be watching that. They're very peasanty, farmer types and she's got a long dress on because he has to lift this dress up. Maybe the animals are standing around. It's always done when she's not expecting it. I've had that one for a while as well. I must have got that from a book; I read it and thought, oh, that's interesting. There's another one where this man is driving in a big car and he picks up this woman to take her to work. Is that right? Let me think, because somehow the wife is left? Then on the way to work they stop and have sex.

My fantasies are very sneaky. It's someone and there's always a wife involved. But it's always rough-and-ready sex. It's never loving sex. There's another fantasy that is really fun – I don't know where I get these from. It's a cloakroom. The man is handing his hat in. The girl is a very prim girl and she's wearing an amazingly short skirt and when she reaches over to put the hat down he somehow or another is there, and again he has her from behind. He unzips his trousers and ... I can bring myself to orgasm in about two minutes. Whereas it would be ages to get an orgasm with a man. Very rarely was it joint orgasm. Because I didn't come. It's much better without a man. I have absolutely no difficulties whatsoever in having an orgasm; once the scene is in my head, it will happen very quickly.

In my fantasies I am always watching. I don't want to be having sex with the men. I didn't watch in my younger life, I participated. I didn't think much either; I just did it. I didn't have any reservations. I'd have a one-night stand if I met somebody at a party. When I look back now, especially being a feminist, I think, how could I? How could I not think for a second about the wives and the women? I took *no* responsibility for that *whatsoever*. None. I thought it didn't matter. There was a way of splitting it in my head. I could have sex with somebody's husband then I would be talking to the wife and be really pally with her. I didn't ever feel guilty. One of the women I was really friendly with, who was such an attractive woman, said, 'You led my husband astray. I thought that was terrible what you did to him.' Looking back I did some terrible things; and my children think I did terrible things. Going off to Mexico for a month and leaving them with somebody I hardly knew. I would sleep with whoever. Maybe I thought so little of myself it didn't matter who I had sex with. Pregnancy, sexually transmitted disease and health didn't seem to be issues then: it was a different world. Once my coil was in I thought, 'Oh my God!' But that would not have stopped me: my sexual feelings were so strong I was just going to do it. I mean, looking back it was the sixties. I think, 'Oh, well, it was the sixties; we did everything in the sixties.' This is an excuse. You know, maybe people didn't.

I did feel social pressure! Very much! Good girls don't have sex. I grew up when everybody did the same: you only had one boyfriend, perhaps two boyfriends, you went to the cinema and then you went to each other's houses and then you got engaged and had presents and then you got married. Nobody was wild – but I think nobody was wild except me. My friend, Anne: one sexual partner in her life. I think, 'Oh my God, how could you not have other partners?' Because it's so attractive. I had a really wild life. Compared to the rest of my family I was wild. So, a lot of sex. About forty men. Compared to my friends in their seventies, that's very, very unusual. I would never tell my children that – they don't want to know about it. And my boys are not at all like that. My two sons are from my first husband and there is not a strong sex drive there. My granddaughters are young – God Almighty, they'd never behave like that. If my granddaughters were doing that, I'd be worried to death about them. Anything might happen. No, I wouldn't want that at all for them.

My adoptive mum and dad were not sexual people.

They didn't have children; I think that was because she had something wrong with her womb. I probably got my sex drive from my birth mother. I went and found my birth mother when I was twenty-seven. She was combing her hair in the car outside her house and I went up to her and I said, 'Hello, I'm your daughter.' She went, 'Oh, you'd better come in then.' She didn't know I was coming. Looking back, that was an attack, because I was angry with her, I didn't know I was angry with her. She gave me this picture of her and my birth father. When I was born my birth father went to see my birth mother in hospital, but then he went up the hill with a gun; he was going to shoot himself. What he actually did was he volunteered to go to Java and was captured by the Japanese and was shot there. So my coming into the world ...

I was in my twenties during the 1960s. The sixties did affect me. In pictures of me in my early twenties at the boys' christenings, you'd think, 'Shirley was middle-aged.' In my early twenties, I *was* middle-aged. When I got divorced that was all thrown off and I was a hippy! I went to university, I was a feminist, I had long earrings, long hair, long loose clothes, sandals, no make-up. In the eighties I went to Greenham Common when my son was a few months old. Feminism didn't affect my sexuality. Not really. But there was a terrific solidarity between the women. Women would visit and not be active but they'd bring a cake or wire cutters and look after my tent while I cut the fence wire, and it's a good job they did because one night while we were out cutting the wires, some drunks from Newbury were going to steal our tent, and the baby was in the tent and he started to cry. There was terrific solidarity; that feeling of being women together was terrific. I believe women are equal to men; that's why I'm a feminist. I'm not keen on injustice and I can see it's still there.

Something in me blossoms when I go to Spain. Two years ago I'm on holiday in Spain at a little place I have there. I'd gone to an open-air classical music concert. I'm sitting next to this man, I've got a wonderful view of the mountains, and he said, 'Are you American?' and I said, '*No!* I'm English!' and then he was just *so* nice. He told me he was a sculptor from Belgium, and I thought, 'Oh my God!' You can imagine. It was just up my street. He speaks French. Oh! That's it. I said, 'Are you coming to the concert tomorrow?' and he said no he wasn't. The next night he came and he was obviously looking for me. Well, I was so girlish, I can't tell you. I was sixteen again. Totally. He's very tall, attractive, sixty-two. Interested in music. And I'm there in my Biba dress with my hair up, waiting for love, I suppose. Crazy. We went for a drink that night. I thought, 'Oh my God, after twenty-five years somebody actually finds me attractive. That's fabulous.'

Then I went to see him in Belgium. This was mad. I obviously haven't changed or learned a thing. Even though nothing much was happening there was something in my head about, 'This could be something ... and it would suit me really well.' He wouldn't have to come here and live with me. I mean, I'm not interested in having someone come and live in my house with me; that's my idea of hell. Can you imagine it? So I had this fantasy, I could go to Belgium every month. And spend a lovely weekend. My sexual fantasy with him was these visions of us having a terrific time. I thought, 'Come to Spain and it will be lovely and warm and we'll go to concerts and we'll have this amazing sex and it will be fantastic.' That's what got me all going and girly.

In Belgium he took me to this hotel he'd booked and the woman presumed we were together and he said, 'I'm not staying! I'm not staying!' Then he told me things like, oh my

God, he suffers with sleep apnoea so he goes to bed with tubes and God knows what, and I thought, 'Oh bother!' I said some really sarcastic things back to him.

My sexuality has changed dramatically over the years. I'm not interested in sex any more – I am interested for myself – but not with someone else. Somebody I know, his wife died and he couldn't live without a woman so he got somebody fifteen years younger than him and I thought, 'Oh my God, I'd *never* consider sleeping with him.' Maybe I just don't want an old man. Maybe I want a young man! I can't imagine meeting somebody I'd like to have sex with now, unless he was forty or fifty and then would he be interested in having sex with me? Therapy helped my self-esteem and now if I had a partner I'd be very fussy. Actually I've been thinking the significant other need not be a man. I wonder if that comes from me not being interested in sex now? A woman would be great. Just a person to share things. And to live with. Separately and together.

The life force is strong in me now. And I think I'm still a bit wild, to tell the truth. I feel wild. Being scared is not a feeling I feel often. I feel it more since getting older. I just breezed through life not knowing much, not thinking much of myself. That has changed.'

# 13

# Muslim

Jannah, 19, west London

*'I don't want him going to Hell because of me'*

'Okay, me. I'm in university in my first year. I'm doing a psychology degree in Westminster University and it was very hard to get there because I've got dyslexia. Shockingly, I got into university. Shocked everyone, pretty much. Then luckily I also found a job in Tesco the same day I started uni. So it was great. That's pretty much my life: uni, work and trying to become a better Muslim.

Let me tell you my story. Before I tried becoming a more better Muslim I actually did have a boyfriend. He was a Muslim. I met him at school, we were like first lovers; we went everywhere together. My mum knew about my boyfriend, pretty much everyone knew about him. But something inside me wasn't feeling right; it wasn't feeling pure enough for me to carry on. Even when I was with him, I tried to become a better Muslim. So then one day after like – how many years? plenty of years... long time – I said to him, 'Okay, listen. I want to become a good Muslim and I want you to be happy with the decision that I'm making and in doing so, I can't be with you any more.' I said that to him. And he was the most proudest person ever. He was so proud, he was like, 'You know what, I'll wait for you, I'll wait for you,' and this and that.

And there were some educations along the way, as I was trying to become a good Muslim. I was thinking to myself, 'I need a husband who is at the same level as me.' So I said to him, 'Listen, for me have a husband I need a practising husband, I need a husband that's a good Muslim,' – not everyone's perfect, don't get me wrong – 'but someone who prays, someone who's God-fearing, who respects other people, someone who's not into smoking, that's not into alcohol,' – not that I'm saying that my ex was, but I just stated that. And because he's not at that same level I said, 'I can't compromise my religion for you. I cannot compromise my heaven for you.' I don't want him sinning over me either. I don't want him going to Hell because of me. Because us having a relationship before marriage is a sin. It's a plain, simple sin.

I wouldn't say we were like crazy intimate. Not like in this society. What we did was dating: eat and spend time together. That's how we were brought up; get to know the person first before you jump into something that you may regret. I'm a human being, life is not all about sex. What we did isn't something I should really expose because that's my past. I repented to God afterwards: 'I'm sorry I was with him.' Allah knows that human beings aren't perfect, but He's just waiting for us to go back to Him and say, 'Allah, forgive me for what I did and I won't do it again.'

When I let go of my boyfriend it was a weight off my shoulders. I did it for a good reason so why would I be heartbroken? I probably missed him slightly but then again it's the Devil playing up: 'You miss him, go back to him.' Same age as me, he's in university. He works. I think he has a car. If he doesn't become a good Muslim I know for a fact if I follow my desires, our personalities would clash. He might want to go out drinking and smoking and I'd be like, 'Look, I don't drink and smoke because I want to please the Lord and preserve myself for you. I don't think so! Not happening.' If he was a good Muslim then it would be okay to be together – *if* we're married. I would just say, 'If you want me, marry me.'

I started to wear the hijab and the abayah when I was seventeen: for everyone it was a shock. The hijab is a long black material and I pin it round my head. I put a little cloth cap underneath first so my baby hairs don't come out. Me, I like mine silk. Black is a simple, beautiful colour. I do wear other colours sometimes but I like to keep it plain and modest. I've gone from fashion colours to more of, 'No, I want to please the Lord instead. More plain, plain, plain, plain, plain.' The hijab is comfortable, and also there are rewards. They say that a drop of sweat on a summer's day is very heavy on the scales of good deeds. So that keeps me content.

Think of a person, right, who is a rapist. If I was to walk past him and another girl in a miniskirt was to walk past him, who do you think he's going to jump on first, realistically? Realistically? The girl that's not covered: he can do something quick, simple, go. So we are protected in that way. We also do this prayer if we feel like we are threatened – for example, if a man is following us then we say the Ayatul Kursi prayer from the Qur'an and normally that works a treat all the time.

Everyone has sexual desires but men have something for women and they can't help but look if they see skin, do you know what I'm saying? We are helping men in a sense:

'You don't have to look; we are covered.' We're covering up so unwanted men cannot see us in that perverse way. We don't cover ourselves because men can't control themselves. No. Men, they can control themselves and God tells them to lower their gaze. It's not, 'Because the men do this, we have to cover up.' Nothing like that. We are valuing ourselves, valuing our beauty, that's the main essence of it. God has honoured the woman, we are so honoured in this life, it's like we are the queens, right? I feel really good as a woman. Well, I value myself. The hijab, right, we see it like this: when you find a pearl, you find it within its shell. My body, my hair, is a pearl so it has to be covered. I cover my head as that's my beauty; I cover my body because that's my beauty. We have to wear the hijab to preserve our beauty because why would we show our beauty to any man?

Say, for instance, I was married now, I could show all my beauty to my husband, even my hair. Then my husband could see everything of me, my this, my that. I can show my hair to other women regardless of them being in my family. I can have any hairstyle I want but I like it long. I look different without the hijab. When my friends suddenly take off their hijabs or I take off mine, it's like, 'Wow!' We say, 'God praise you because you're so beautiful, God made you so beautiful.' And why would we share that with the world when it's so precious and so valuable?

I would have an arranged marriage. I can get married whenever I want but I told my parents, 'Personally,' I said, 'after my degree. I would prefer to get married slightly early so I can spend time with my husband before there's any kids in the future.' I'm a bit of a traditional sort of girl. My mum was married when she was seventeen. An arranged marriage. In Bangladesh. Happily married. She's now a housewife, house mum, amazing mum. Two older brothers. And my dad is a waiter at the moment. He did education back home in Bangladesh but when my mum got him here he didn't carry on with the education because he had kids. My dad, he's a smart man but he had to work straight away but he did a grand job, my dad.

I trust my mum. It's not like she's going to pick someone from a list and be like, 'That's it, you're going to get married.' It's nothing like that. It's more like, 'Oh, look, Jannah, I've found someone for you, would you like to look into it?' I will ask questions to the person, like 'So what do you do as your daily life? What are your goals in life?' And be mindful what questions I'm asking because they're going to be my soul mate. I have to see whether we match. Islam teaches us that love starts from marriage. You're getting to know that person from *marriage*, nothing beforehand. Beforehand you will have desires – don't get me wrong, you will – but God will see what you do with those desires. God gives us a way to deal with them so either you get married, you can do that – get married if you're having those extreme feelings. Instead of getting into a relationship that is sin, just get married. It's fine. Or you can fast. It's good for the body as a whole, even scientifically. God says if you can't marry, you fast and that helps the body control the sexual desires.

Human beings and animals all have sexual desires, right? But God has taught us to value ourselves and discipline ourselves, because we're not going to show our bum and this and that because that's relating yourself to an animal. The men are told to lower their gaze. The first glimpse – okay, God has forgiven him. Don't take the second glimpse, respect that woman the way she is. Don't take her as meat. They're persuaded to lower their head, walk past, giving the woman space and respect. The same for a woman. If I find someone amazingly attractive, obviously I saw him once to figure out that he is attractive! Me, I wouldn't look again. Say, for instance, I found someone *so* good-looking, I wouldn't burst out, 'Oh my God! He's so hot!' No! It's not something I ponder over. Like, 'Oh, I find someone attractive, oh, now I'm thinking about being intimate with them.' It's nothing like that.

I wouldn't say that I don't have sexual feelings, that wouldn't make me human. It's what I do with them. I don't follow my sexual desires because that doesn't lead me anywhere. I carry on with my life because I've got other things to think about: God gave me praying times, I pray five times a day so my life is really busy. Sexual stuff, that all comes after marriage. When I'm married I can have sexual thoughts about my husband. Yeah. It's my husband. Obviously! Yeah.

I'm looking forward to getting married. Yeah, such a blessing. God has already written who I'm going to get married to. I want a good-looking man! No, I'm not really into looks; personality wins me over, definitely. Has to be funny, because I also have a character, I'm very boisterous and very naughty and cheeky, trust me, I have this cheekiness in me. I was such a naughty kid. When I was a child I had behavioural problems. I used to get into fights, had a foul mouth, trust me, honestly. Because I was very small, other kids used to provoke me, they didn't know this little monster was inside me, so I would bark back. My parents were like, 'You can't be naughty all the time; we can't always collect you early from school.' And you know, I never used to listen. Never used to listen. Then something hit me and I just had to change. And since I was trying, and when I was praying, my life kind of pieced together. My religion grounded me and changed me into a completely different person. When it comes to my religion I can be very passionate.

My goodness! I am passionate and full of peace and tranquillity. I would never jeopardise my heaven for anything really.

I am telling you, this society is too sexualised. I hear about one-night stands, and where's the human being in that? Where are human beings going? Back in the days, even Western culture had the tradition to get married first, of sex after marriage. Women give it too easy for the men to grab them and do whatever to them. They need to protect themselves, they need to value themselves and find a man who's going to protect them and value them for who they are, not for what they have.

I think of myself as English. Yeah, why not? I was born here. I am Muslim more than anything. I do feel free as a Muslim woman but there are times when I go outside and I do get abused, especially around the city. Many times. Vans drive past, and they say names or 'you bomber', and 'terrorist'. I've got a traditional Asian culture behind me and I've also got the Muslim culture around me. I'm surrounded by one value system but live in a different one. I know I have a few values that are different from others, but I don't think any less of Western women. No way. I cannot even think that ... It would be a sin if I looked any less at someone. You and me are human at the end of the day. Not everything is about men for me. My goodness, that would make me like ...! No, not everything is about me. Everything is about, 'How can I make myself a better Muslim.' The *main* thing when I do something is I have to say, 'How do I please the Lord?'

# 14

# Student

Anna, 19, Windsor

*'In exam time recently I've had this feeling, "I want to be whipped!"'*

'My necklace is a black leather strap with a silver heart padlock on. That's a symbol of submission and ownership. I keep the key; my boyfriend has the other key. My colleague in the shop I work in recognised it when I came into work wearing it! She said, 'Oh! Has William given you a collar?' and I was like, 'Yes!' I was really pleased because she's someone I talk with very openly about sexuality and it was nice for me to have that reaffirmed. I *like* talking openly about this stuff because people don't! There's a lot of stigma attached to sex. You have a big dichotomy, particularly with women, between: Do you have sex? Do you not? Do you be a slut? Do you be a virgin? Do you be a prude? Do you be a man-whore? You can't really win. All of these give a very negative impression of sex. And it's a *good* thing to have sex; it's a good thing to be intimate with someone.

I discovered BDSM by accident on a creative-writing website. I came to this story; it was like, 'WARNING: BDSM', and a list of sex acts. I was like, 'I don't know what these are. I'm just going to read them.' I was like, 'This is like really interesting!' I was thirteen years old and it was a huge revelation for me. BDSM is bondage, discipline, dominance, submission, sadomasochism. Just kind of like, 'I didn't know this existed.' I was *very* attracted to *a lot* of women at that time. Still am.

I turned eighteen in March, I waited until my A-level exams were done, and in June I went to my first BDSM gathering. It was in Windsor. It was just a social gathering: we met up in a pub, got to know each other. There are loads of BDSM gatherings up in the north, which is brilliant because I can go to them at university *and* not have to lie to Mother about where I am! My mum doesn't know what my relationship is like!

I met my boyfriend at my first event. Which was a bit of a surprise. I went in going, 'Right, first of all I'm a lesbian,' because I'd only ever been attracted to women. Then I was like, 'Wait a minute! This is a guy! I kind of like this guy! Whoops!' A few weeks later we ended up getting together. We're getting on for a year now. Which is lovely. And obviously I went off to university at the end of the summer and then we kept it going. He's twenty-eight and I go down to Windsor to see him.

Now I really like whips. My boyfriend got *really* into whips, and I was just like, 'Okay, I'll try it!' And then I *really* enjoyed it. He's got a proper good whip: oh, it's a proper whip. It's four foot long. It's black and leather and got a little silver – I've completely forgotten what the technical term is for it – on the handle. He's just bought a dressage whip in a sports shop. So *that's* going to be interesting.

It hurts. *Yeah.* Part of the pleasure is that it hurts. It hurts a lot. Yep! Though it doesn't hurt me as much as it could. I tend to find there's a thing called subspace and when I am submitting to my boyfriend I go into a slightly altered state of consciousness. When I'm in subspace it hurts but nowhere near as much. I don't cry because I get a lot of endorphins and adrenaline and it feels really good but when I'm coming back to reality then I can cry if I'm really stressed or emotional. I get a little bit embarrassed but my boyfriend is *lovely* about it, he just hugs me and lets me come down. That's aftercare, looking after who's been involved. For me it's giving hugs. Basically just hugs. And cuddles. When I'm coming out of it I shake because I have all this adrenaline in my system. Occasionally I need to eat something really sugary so I actually keep sweets in my bag if I'm ever going round to my boyfriend's house.

I do it whenever I get the chance. My boyfriend's room is tiny! Somehow we manage to do it. We just about have enough width in his flat in Windsor to do it front-on. In my university bedroom we do it side-on rather than front-on, which is kind of irritating because one side of me gets a lot heavier hit than the other side. Whipping is quite loud! Once my flatmates were playing loud music so we thought we'd irritate them, cracked the whip around my room a bit. Just for fun.

Beating turns me on sexually. I haven't got an orgasm from being whipped but I know people who do. It does hurt – but I don't mind! The thing I really like about whips is I *love* having marks; I *love* having something to show for it. I like taking pictures of myself, and admiring myself. It's usually just the back of my legs from my knees to my bottom. I generally keep it hidden, particularly when I'm at home with my parents. How long my skin takes to heal depends. When I use the whip on bare skin I get marks down my thighs. My thighs take a lot longer to heal up; a couple of weeks. My bum is usually healed in a week or so. I've never had to have medical care before. I've got Arnica cream if I bruise and antiseptic plasters if my skin cuts open accidentally. That would only ever be by accident. I know people who play to that level regularly but that's not something I'm at yet. It's one of my boyfriend's limits as well.

My closest friend loves showing off all her marks. It's *brilliant*, I love it! She gets *so* excited about it and it's really lovely, actually. She's just gotten engaged to the guy who she does it with. They're *really* sweet and she *really* loves him and it's really, really sweet to see. He would break the skin. He's twenty-six and she has just turned twenty-three. She's graduating this year; he graduated a few years ago. They are getting married in a couple of years.

There's a thing called hard limits. Hard limits are things you won't do. Soft limits are things you could push. Blood is on my hard list. Blood means anything that draws blood, so it could be cutting or being hit so hard you draw blood; it could be needles. You insert needles into the skin; it's a masochistic thing. I've seen some *really* gorgeous patterns made by coloured needles put though the skin on people's backs. It's really beautiful but it makes me shudder. The needles are inserted sideways in and out, like sewing without thread. A couple of my friends who'd just got engaged were doing needles at a demonstration and he was like, 'Hey, Anna, do you want come and watch us?' And I was like, 'Okay, I'm kind of curious.' She had three needles stuck sideways into her arm and then he was taking them out of her arm and the sight of that made me nearly faint! Don't do needles. She was in pain. She likes it – she's *very* masochistic, she loves everything like that.

Also on my hard limits list is anything illegal like bestiality, under-age sex, that's like – no. Another big one I have is verbal humiliation – I won't do that. It's basically verbally degrading someone. I had a very bad experience with it and I'm not going anywhere near that. I vaguely knew him; his girlfriend was a friend of mine. It was last October, my second week of university. I said the safe word: he didn't stop. So that crossed into sexual assault territory. It wasn't a good experience for me. It took me a long time to talk about it because my memory was blurred; I didn't know what happened, and there was a high possibility that my drink was spiked with drugs because afterwards I needed to stick a lot of the pieces together from that night. It's been good for me to actually talk about it. Now I'm getting it out there and it feels better.

I know people who get sexual pleasure from being in pain, and have orgasms. I've seen this girl have orgasms through being whipped. Having said that, her boyfriend has trained her to orgasm on command so she can't actually orgasm unless he tells her that she can. It's by hypnotism and conditioned responses – it's fascinating and I *love* watching them do it. He's got a trigger to make her be still, which is running a finger along her eyebrow. He does that and she will go completely still. She can't do anything. She's *very* aware of everything happening around her but she can't do anything about it. To stop her being completely still, he kisses her. He loves tickling people to irritate them and he's now got her conditioned to feel the sensation of tickling when he says certain stuff to her. He's done it at social events before. It's really funny! She gets really irritated at him. Usually she just hits him on the arm.

I've played with them as a couple privately in their homes, a kind of open relationship kind of thing. They're like, 'Hey! Come round to our house. We'll hit you!' And I'm just like, 'Okay!' The man will hit – can be hand, paddles, canes, hairbrush, ruler, floggers. Floggers are similar to whips but they're multi-tailed, heavy. You can do fancy stuff, like twist them. It's quite artsy, interesting flogging. When my boyfriend came up to stay we got the floggers out – he's done a lot of circus skills before – and the four of us were playing and it was really fun. Last time there was a foursome on the cards; we never got round to it, we were all tired. But yeah, I would be fine with a foursome. We haven't reached that point yet of my boyfriend and I having sex with someone else. We operate a policy of, 'Do what you want, just tell each other.' But not in front of each other, not yet.

I wasn't whipped as a child. I was raised very normally. As a child I had a fantasy of being whipped. Definitely! My boyfriend said the scene in *Aladdin* where Jasmine gets chained up – he liked that. For me it was watching *Thunderbirds* because Lady Penelope always got tied up! At school we would re-enact *Thunderbirds* scenes and I always wanted to be Lady Penelope.

I have been the youngest at pretty much every event I have been to. I don't look like I'm into BDSM. I get that a lot! A lot of people say that to me. I look young and innocent. That's what it is. It's something people don't expect from me and it's kind of hilarious when I end up being open about it, because it defies what the expectation is. Most of the submissives I know are either *very* young, so twenty-five or below, or *very* old: fifty or above. But then I can't speak for everyone. It's very much in my nature to be submissive. Yeah. I was talking with my boyfriend: our personality traits are very similar. We're both people-pleasing, supportive people, we want to take care and protect. Because I'm a people pleaser, I like making someone else feel happy. But our traits manifest themselves in different ways: him being dominant and me being submissive, it's the same thing.

I have had fantasies and acted them out. So if my boyfriend says something then we'll do it. Or I'll say something. He had a schoolgirl fetish so he was like, 'I'd like to see you in a pair of long white socks.' I was like, 'Okay. I'm just going the whole hog.' I got long white socks. I had a short kilt and a white button-down shirt. Turned up at his house, hair in pigtails. It was great! It was *really* good. It's nice to be able to fulfil those fantasies.

My fantasies tend to be very nameless, faceless, but a lot of them are based on my experiences now, so I can feel touch, I can hear things. I have audio clips of people stored in my head so I can actually hear my boyfriend saying a particular sentence ... it's quite nice actually. Just the enclosure that it brings, being private and being able to feel things. I usually just start masturbating and see what comes, preferably me!

Sometimes I feel I really want to be whipped. Particularly when I'm stressed, or I'm anxious or I'm nervous. In exam time recently I've been feeling, 'I want to be whipped! I want to be whipped!' because it's stress-relieving for me, it's cathartic, it lets me get rid of negativity and emotions so it's healthy for me to do it. I like it and it's just a good thing for me to do because it makes me feel better in myself. So yeah, I do get that urge *quite* a lot. When I first started I couldn't take *anywhere* near as much the level of impact of whips, hands, floggers, tying, spanking as I can now, which is a personal achievement for me. It makes me feel proud of myself that I can do it.

I'm definitely a feminist. I really am. I have a big feminist view on people being sexually empowered, people not feeling shame about sex – within reason and the law. From BDSM I get a *huge* amount of self-esteem, I get self-worth, I feel good about myself and I can feel proud of something I've achieved. Female submissive is a very worn-down stereotype. Feminists, when they've opposed this stuff, say if you have a male dominant and a female submissive you're reinforcing patriarchal values. But a, that's heterosexist, b, that implies all women are submissive, c, who cares? They are doing what they want to do in bed, what does it matter? Heterosexist means that you're implying that all couples are heterosexual, so you can't include gay or lesbian couples. I don't feel I'm acting out heterosexual value systems.

Submission is very empowering, it gives me a lot of confidence; it makes me feel like I have something to be proud of. I do it because I like doing it. I do it because I feel good doing it, I feel sexually empowered doing it, because I've made the choice to submit to him by my own consent because that's what *I* want and it's what he wants. There's nothing less empowering about submitting than being dominant. As long as I have made the choice to do it, that's what's empowering, it's not what I'm doing.

When I was masturbating when I was younger, because I had no sexual experience, I had nothing to go on so I was just thinking about the physical sensations. I didn't know about gay people. I learned about it when I was twelve, I didn't initially apply the term to myself; I was just like, 'Okay, that's cool, that stuff exists.' I didn't actually label myself as a lesbian until I was seventeen. I waited to develop, to make sure that was what I was secure in. I told my parents when I was sixteen. My mum was lovely about it; I wouldn't have expected any different, but then it was about me being able to be comfortable with it myself before I told anyone else. My parents are conventional for the most part. My childhood was very conventional. My school – as lovely as it was, I had a *brilliant* time there – liked to think it was a lot more liberal than it was. It was an all-girls' private school in the Home Counties.

We started Sex Education in Year 5 when we were ten years old. We got the period talk, Year 6 we got another period talk and a bit of talk about the changes boys go through during puberty. Year 7 we got a period talk. Year 8 we got a period talk. It was just literally periods all your life! Then in Year 9 they tried to do contraception with us and failed because the teacher was known throughout the school as a joke teacher. None of us liked her. It didn't go well, we spent most of the lesson playing Wink Murder behind her back because she made us all sit in a circle on the floor around her, bearing in mind at this point we are fourteen-year-old girls who do not want to sit cross-legged on the floor while someone goes 'This is a condom' at us. And that was about it. There was a lot of hesitation about anything that involved affection between two girls. We didn't learn about sexuality, it didn't get a mention. I've educated myself.

At eighteen, school was the only experience I'd had. I'd spent my life being surrounded by girls and beautiful women – that was what I was used to. So that's what I'd based all my sexual fantasies on. My boyfriend was the first person I'd ever kissed. Before, most of my fantasy was women. I thought I was a lesbian. I've been pleasantly surprised. I definitely still have stronger feelings for women than I do men, but I'm *very* happy with my boyfriend.

My boyfriend works in retail. Perfectly normal guy. He's very open about it with his work colleagues. Yeah. He shows them pictures of me. I'm okay with that. I'm fine! I really don't mind! The general atmosphere where he works is very open and very dirty-humour-based, which probably fits in quite nicely. My boyfriend's family knows. My boyfriend's parents didn't discover he was into this, he discovered his parents were into it. He found photographs and a book of Victorian discipline under their bed when he was sixteen. I've met them; they are perfectly normal people. They know *exactly* what our relationship is, which I'm fine with. If his parents are comfortable with that then I have no issue with that either.

I've always felt I should be able to talk about these things. Even today, female masturbation is a bit of a taboo and it *shouldn't* be: it's normal, it's healthy, it's what people should do, it makes you learn about your own body and what you want. My experience of *not* having been told about this stuff makes me want to talk about it: about being gay, about sex, about relationships, about everything, because I didn't know about it so other people probably don't know. And I definitely want to continue with BDSM. I've met so many good people; I have so many close friends through doing it. I really enjoy it. Do I want to do BDSM in the long term? Yeah.'

## 15

# Mother

Yvette, 48, Crewe

*'Do you remember the Turkish Delight ads?'*

'When I was very young, eighteen and a half, I had this boyfriend called Glenn. I was living in America away from my family and he was really into pornography, heavy-duty porn. I'd never come across anyone like this before – well, the man upstairs used to have porn mags and me and my brother used to look at them. This guy, Glenn, used to take me to – oh my God – the tackiest hotels with hot tubs and mirrors on the ceilings and, being young and not knowing that much about the world, I used to watch these really horrible – maybe they weren't really horrible, maybe they were okay – films with him to be grown up, then have sex under the mirrors. I tried to be grown up and do all that stuff and watch films but one time I thought, 'Oh God, I'm sick and bloody tired of listening to people making noises.' Finally I agreed I would watch the films if he turned the sound down because the sound was like, 'Ugh, so tedious'. It did *nothing* for me. I pretended it did at first. When I was a child my parents went on about what a great movie *Deep Throat* was, saying, 'Oh, it's such a great film, it's kind of intellectual and funny.' I said to this guy, 'Okay, I'll watch *Deep Throat* with you; that's supposed to be good.' Fucking hell! It was such a load of bollocks. Intellectual it wasn't. Funny? Possibly. Dated? Yes. Pornography? Yes. None of it did anything for me at all.

I don't have many memories of my childhood. Well, I do. There was growing up with my mum and my stepfather who were *incredibly* sexual in front of us, snogging, and he was always touching her inappropriately. It became apparent they had a very lustful relationship – he was quite lascivious towards her, and she obviously used her sexuality. It made me feel sick and I considered it dirty, you know, like dirty old men in the seventies. It was disgusting. I vowed I never wanted to be like my mother and as a result I've gone the other way.

I did have an experience with my mum's really close friend, whom I adored. This guy, Keith, whom I loved, was gay. He did come into my bed when I was nine. And I have to say, to say he raped me is far too dramatic, but something happened. I wouldn't even say it was unpleasant. It wasn't horrible. I didn't hate him for it; in fact, I loved him desperately. And it was only a one-off. People say, 'Oh, you should hate him.' Well, I didn't hate him.

He bought me a ladybird orchestra. I liked little things, like little teddies and ornaments, as small girls do. It was tiny ladybirds all playing instruments with a ladybird conductor, and I still have it to this day and it's on display in one of my children's bedrooms. He gave it to me as a way of saying sorry and I still have it and that is probably really screwed up and I don't care. Then my sister said to me a year ago, 'I've got some things of yours,' and it was a birthday card from this man I'd saved because I loved him so much – he's dead now. He died of AIDS. I honestly don't feel any hatred towards him: it's my parents I hate for doing what they did, acting out all their nonsense in front of me. With Keith it was just something that happened. Of course, I never told anyone but it did physically damage me rather badly because I had to go to the doctor on numerous occasions, which is quite sad actually. It really damaged me physically. I didn't make the connections until I was an adult.

I've been married twenty years and have sex with my husband but it's very safe sex. Once, and this is a real secret, my husband wanted me – oh, I feel so bad – when we had sex he wanted me to say things like, 'I want you,' and 'I want you to fuck me,' – rude, rude words as I see it. I'm not a prude, but I just couldn't. It felt really abusive to have to say, 'Oh, fuck me!' It turned him on but there was no way on God's earth to allow myself to do that, it was too physically painful. It's not painful in my vagina, just in my heart; it feels sad, a bit like grief. It's such a mish-mash. Well, this is rather personal and private: sex has always been quite difficult until my body has been overtaken with the physical sensation. Sex has been great when the sensation takes over and obliterates the other feelings and the thinking.

We used to have sex much more often, say twice a week, now it's once every couple of weeks, which probably could be more often. But with the kids and work it's hard to make time for it. I generally don't want to do it; it's something that I feel I ought to do because that's what women do. I've got nothing to prove – I've had four children. I can get pregnant; I've had babies. I love babies, but no more do I want to give birth to them so there's no meaning in that department. It's sort of my marital duty but when I *do* do it, I do enjoy it. Because I don't want any more kids there's no incentive to get pregnant.

Never in my life have I masturbated! Ever! That I know is weird. Sex with myself – are you joking? Urh – no. My husband said to me about fifteen years ago, 'Maybe you should just try,' but the idea is horrendous because it's so dirty and not nice. It's not physically dirty, obviously: I'm quite a clean person. It's so not what I can do. Oh, it's so painful I don't even know how to go there. I bought a book about healing from sexual abuse and there was this one exercise where you had to lay on the floor and clench your buttocks and touch yourself very gently and I vowed to myself I might try that but I never have!

If I allow myself to think about what I want I freeze over and I can't go there. That's why I've never had a sexual fantasy. I'd be far too scared to. I fantasise more about winning the lottery, which is completely unlikely to happen, especially as I don't buy lottery tickets. Sometimes I think it would be lovely to have an affair with a man who completely adored me and bought me presents *all* the time but that's more of a Prince Charming fantasy coming to rescue me from my life and bringing me money. Obviously, I fancy men and think, 'That'd be nice,' or, 'He's handsome,' but I'd never be like a sadomasochistic person or a person who wants to sleep with two people at once, or goes to those parties where they put their keys in the bowl on the table. No, I've never fancied that, never even allowed myself to. Then I turn into my grandmother who, if we watched anything on telly and there was even a vague bit of kissing, she'd close her eyes. I remember watching *Carry on Camping* with her and she was muttering away. She was Dutch and she was tutting in these funny Dutch words and I was feeling really ashamed that I thought *Carry on Camping* was funny.

I probably could do with some therapy but the idea of talking about this stuff fills me with *absolute* dread so I've avoided it like the plague. I'd like to look at it but I'm really nervous in that I don't want to have a sort of mini breakdown. I think, 'Oh my God! What if I die an old lady and I've never sorted this stuff out?' And part of me thinks, 'Well, I don't care. It's too painful.' But then maybe my life would be better; I don't know. It would be lovely to be able to explore myself, not masturbate-explore, but explore that side of myself. Because men do find me very attractive. I still get men bloody chatting me up and it really annoys me. I'm always getting blokes chatting me up and they're always really ugly. They're never the gorgeous businessmen who on a train journey happen to say, 'Oh, look, I happen to have a diamond ring, you don't have to give me anything,' and then I can go off and sell it and pay my PhD fees and no one would know!

My children are teenagers. It's been strange because I grew up in a house where my stepfather would walk around naked with an erection, and I had *no* privacy at all. If I was in the bath he would walk in and look at me and even took photos of me. Then to have children who suddenly start shutting the door ... When they were little we would all have baths together and it was so lovely – me in the bath with their little gorgeous beautiful bodies and then suddenly my daughter didn't want to get in the bath with me and she wanted her own space and I had to respect that. I didn't like it. The same has happened with every single one of them – I have to respect their privacy. It's a shame that my daughter doesn't let me see her body naked. I feel sad that I can't go and chat to her in the bath, but she doesn't want me to so I can't. And the boys, well that would be totally inappropriate, and that's that.

I was walking through the park today with the dog and I

saw this piece from a magazine on the ground and I looked at it and thought, 'They're really pornographic images.' I thought, 'Gosh, I'd hate my sons to see this. I'm going to pick it up.' There were these images of women with their legs spread showing different aspects of their vaginas. There were eight of them and they were so different, and if I was a little boy and I saw that I would probably be really taken aback so I threw it in the bin.

The first time I looked at my vagina was after I had my third child. I had never allowed myself to look at any of my private parts – my private parts! I was really shocked at how it looked. I remember saying to the midwife, 'Is it unusual? Would you mind having a look?' She said, 'It looks fine, that's how they look after childbirth.' But these vaginas in the park looked like something I'd never seen before in my life. Maybe if they'd been photographed in a different way they could look absolutely beautiful but the hard photography of women showing their legs and their vaginas felt like objectification of women – it didn't feel right and I'm glad I picked up that piece of porn and put it in the bin. Having grown up with not being allowed to explore one's own body and self, it was such a bastardisation of the women – of women.

Sex is such a fragile thing and sexuality needs to be nurtured and grown, not cut off or stamped on. Had mine been allowed to be nurtured and grow I wouldn't be in the position that I am now; someone who's scared to have a sexual fantasy, who thinks it's dirty, who thinks it's scary, who thinks it's rude! Yeah. Rude and not ladylike and not nice, which I know intellectually is not right.

Do you remember those Turkish Delight ads when we were little girls? It was on ITV in the 1970s back in the day when to be an Arab was mystical. It would say, 'Fry's Turkish

Delight' and a lady would come on and she'd say, 'Full of Eastern promise'. There she was looking gorgeous and in the background was some Omar Sharif-type Arab in a tent on a sand dune. I suppose the nearest thing as a child I got to a sexual fantasy was the idea of being like the Fry's Turkish Delight lady with my veil and the handsome Arab sheik in the background. That's as far as it went. There would be no other encounter other than him whisking me off to a tent full of wonderful purple and red silk cushions. Oh God – I bet some women have really juicy, interesting sexual fantasies and mine is the Fry's Turkish Delight advert!'

# 16

# Slut

May, 37, Liverpool

*'Ethical slut! That's what I want to be'*

'I associate water with sexuality. I will masturbate and I'm bringing myself to orgasm and I'll imagine the sea as my lover. I might become the sea: I *am* the element that the sea is, powerful but soft, moving, watery. I close my eyes and imagine how the sea touches me as I lie in it or lie on the beach as it starts to come up me, then it's splashing me and then how it takes my breath away. I'm imagining *gorgeous*, delicious feelings and breathing in the way that I would when I'm relaxing and completely surrendered to the sea, *despite* its power to kill or drown me, so I have trust. It's a sensual imagining.

Eco-sexuality is a new name for – I'm going to put a stab in the dark – enjoying the sensuousness of nature. Kids do it a lot, human beings do it, animals do it. We bask in the sun or enjoy the deliciousness of water or the smell of a flower.

We say we are kissed by the sun. Eco-sexuality is not getting a stick and shoving it inside me. If I've been feeling jangly I've gone – this sounds a bit hippy – 'Go to nature and *be* in nature.' I've gone, 'What element do I want? I really want long grass tickling me.' And I'll go and do that. The idea of instead of Earth Mother, it's Earth Lover. It's allowing nature to be my lover.

Polyamorous is something I am in the world. Polyamory is acknowledging that I can be in love with many different people at one time. And yes, I might be having sex with them as well, but it's about love. I did have a three-way relationship where I was in love with the female and the male and all three of us were equal. It was amazing. It was idyllic. I had a sexual relationship with her as well as him. We all had sex together. Me and the male engaged with each other first and expressed our attraction during a six-month course we were on. I had a similar experience with the female over the same course and this was one of the very first female–female experiences I'd had. We said – because we all had mutual attraction – let's see if we'd enjoy a threesome.

It was like heaven on earth. I mean it; I *really* mean it. It was *so* conscious. We brought our fears and vulnerabilities; he was like, 'I've got performance anxiety.' A lot of our fears were, 'Is my dream actually going to come true now?' Because I'd not imagined what it would be like to do this not drunk, not like, 'Oh, we just ended up doing it, because we were in the hot tub.' We chose to do it; we planned it. We sat in a triangle cross-legged and spoke honestly, we did a check-in first and then we were like, 'What shall we do?' We played with some exercises with one person asking for whatever they wanted. It was sensuality, not just sex or 'I want you to suck this, and do that.' It was like, 'I want you to hold me, and let me cry like I'm eight.' It was absolutely honest. We said twenty minutes each doing exercises and then we allowed the alchemy of whatever.

We've done it lots. We've had other lovers and been separate and then we come back at different times, spontaneously. All three of us are still in acknowledgement that we *love* and are attracted to each other. We are lovers on and off, here and there. I absolutely love group sharing. Multiple partners at the same time – that's definitely been where I've felt the most joy, connection and calmness. 'Ethical slut' is a brilliant, brilliant phrase. That's what I want to be, what has allegedly been a slut. Not having to cross my legs. But ethical, so it's not, 'I'm just gonna shag whoever and it doesn't matter.'

There are orgies going on in England. There's a great night I've been to in London with at least a hundred people, which used to be called The Sex Maniacs' Ball and now is called The Night of the Senses. It is a sex club encouraging able-bodied to mix with disabled-bodied people, especially around sexuality. I *love* that concept. Because unfortunately our society creates this model of what is sexy, and, being in a wheelchair, having one leg, having Tourette's, der, der, der, is *right* down the list: they don't have a sexuality and don't want sex. And it's really horrible. It's a real problem. In society everyone is allowed to be sexual apart from disabled people. And the mentally ill.

It's very difficult to literally *be* sexual with lots of people at once but I've been in orgy situations where there have been ten to twenty people in a room. In the Night of the Senses I was in a room where all bits of bodies were touching – a mass. I certainly wasn't having sex with all twenty of them. There was mutual understanding and a group intention, like a crowd watching a concert. That night was great. It had an etiquette booklet and I *love* that about the polyamory community:

there's an agreed etiquette around things like protection. Because it's on the table there's so much more awareness and upfrontness.

There's a thing called sex magic. I've been in a ritual in England where a marquee full of people were all crescendoing in a very long ritual to orgasm at the same time, including men, although the men did not necessarily ejaculate. It was sixty people orgasming at once to create what they wanted. It wasn't like we were all trying to get the same thing. We told a partner what our intention was and we checked a year later, and mine did happen! Yeah. Mine was about the relationships I wanted, and it came into being. I don't know if it's magic because we 'make' things happen too the rest of the year. Since learning about sex magic, when I masturbate, I'm careful what I think about when this powerful energy is passing through me; if I think something negative, the way I'm thinking potentially locks into my cellular system and I might be creating that. Sexuality is our intimate, creative energy because that's how we make babies. You don't have to make a baby with it – you can make anything with it! Of course, the scientists are all going, 'Shut up, May,' and the scientist in me goes, 'Shut up.' Sex magic is the *idea* that you or a whole group of people can create something positive together through sex while in orgasm. It might be a sense of happiness and joy and love, or peace in the world.

In polyamorous communities you could very easily have an experience and be totally put off for life because there's some guy and he owns five women. I struggled with that. Then there are polyamorous communities where drugs and alcohol are fine and it's more about hedonism, whereas I'm not interested in unconscious sex at all. It doesn't do anything for me if I don't feel the connection and I don't see something in his eyes. I'm really into being present. When I was twenty-two I stopped taking drugs, smoking and drinking, not as some weird puritanical thing. It was about being conscious and honest with myself, and being authentic in the world.

Background: Catholic, Scottish father, English mother. Victorian. But a strange mix because my parents have good jobs in medicine. The body in our household was a medical body so it was weirdly acceptable. That did – thankfully – counter all the shame in terms of Catholicism, of 'Keep your legs together.' Without it ever being explicitly written anywhere in the Catholic Church I heard the message loud and clear – and I know my sisters did too – girls don't masturbate. It's bad and it's wrong. It deeply influenced my early years, but that doesn't mean I didn't do it. Catholicism covertly teaches stuff to women, like the body is intrinsically sinful. I *absolutely* believe the opposite, that the body is a wonderful, potentially spiritual vessel of unity and blood and mess, and all the fleshy things are magnificent and to be revelled in as we would a waterfall, not 'Ew, periods! Er, facial hair.' The *power* of the female is often pushed down, and sex in the Catholic Church is only allowed once you are married and even then it's not talked about. Sex is certainly not the place of creativity or joining in union.

Also I went to a girls' school where I didn't have someone say directly, 'You're a slut because you didn't cross your legs,' but I got those subtle messages that if you don't cross your legs you're a slut. English women have a reputation of being reserved and uptight; actually behind closed doors we're outrageous. We just close the doors, shut the curtains and keep the blinds down. To be honest, I'm worried about how in the modern culture, sex is being learned from pornography. In a way you almost couldn't define it as English sexuality, because it's a global milieu from anywhere.

I've never had a great relationship with pornography. That's all porn is: it's friction sex. And her being able to orgasm immediately – that doesn't quite fit with reality. Porn sends me into low self-esteem about my body. As a trained actor, most porn doesn't work for me because I really appreciate very good acting in films, and good plots! Although I have compassion for the young males who are trying to figure out female biology by watching porn. In comparison to men's biology, female biology is like 'Wow!' Having done stuff around female anatomy I really get how 'Wow, this is tricky to figure out.' It's complex, it's mysterious, it's culturally mysterious, and in our culture the woman doesn't know herself that well. Compassion is really important because everyone's got their stuff around sex so if you really want to connect with someone, come with compassion, not expectations.

I'm about to go to a community in Greece which explores polyamory and the idea that ownership over another is a kind of violence that creates, on a bigger scale, a lack of peace in the world. Jealousy and believing that you own your partner, especially male to female, even on a subtle level, creates separation. In the past you did legally own your partner, she was your property. That meant horrific things like beating your wife was legal. And that's violence. And that's so recent.

I love to be talked to in my ear or even someone breathing in my ear; that *absolutely* opens me and I get really juicy and turned on. Another woman might like to be entered really quickly. Most women I know need a lot more than just being shoved into. There's loads of science about this that is thankfully happening. I know this Urban Tantra teacher in New York who is able to bring herself to orgasm just through breathing, no touching of herself at all. A scientist was intrigued by this and put her in a CT scan to see if it was indeed true and not her telling herself it was an orgasm. All the right things were firing up and more.

Honesty is one of the top aphrodisiacs. Yeah! If I'm making love to myself I feel much more comfortable if I'm in my truth: am I tired and trying to help myself go to sleep? Another level of truth might be, 'In my fantasy I'm trying to engage with being hot and sassy,' instead of being in the moment and going, 'Okay, I'm in this room, I'm in a bed and feeling a bit grotty so how about I be with feeling a bit grotty? What would that be like?' That's honesty with myself. That feeds into how I am with sex. I can come to my sexual partner with 'Hi, I'm all ready and preened,' and that might not be true for the moment. I might feel really animal and non-verbal and that doesn't match the partner who's going, 'Do you mind if you wear some underwear?' while I'm growling, 'I don't even know what underwear is! Because I'm like this ball of sexual something, I'm not even a human being any more.' At other times I'm very much, 'I've just come home from work and I want to have nine-to-five sex.' I'm the person that I am in the office.

I remember once I had a lovely time masturbating. I was imagining a swimming pool filled with melted chocolate – because if I'm going to fantasise I'm going to go for it, I'm going to make something that can't be made in the world. So, a swimming pool full of melted chocolate. There were *gorgeous* people and then the swimming pool transformed into the sea so it was warm and then it was cool and sparkly. Bubbling warm chocolate, hot. Yeah. *All* encompassing. Then it was inside me, outside me, I could eat it. Hello! Great. So my fantasy is *not* a plumber knocked on my door, and *oops!* some clothes fell off and we had sex. That plot doesn't work for me. Fantasies can be very much, 'Try to picture a black man walking down the beach towards me and then he grabs hold of me.' But rather than picturing a black male, I might feel the sense of strong arms around me; I imagine the feeling of it as opposed to needing to have a face.

My other fantasy is all the lovers I've ever had or have, I bring them all together for a wonderful orgy. That's one of my favourites. If I've been lovers with someone essentially they're my lover forever in my heart and I don't go, 'Ergh, you're now repulsive to me.' Most of my lovers are still attractive to me. So they're very welcome in my fantasies. I really like the idea of making love to one lover while another is watching. And the lovers obviously all get along fine. In my mind! Of course, *I'm* the centre of attention. It's a very conscious loving orgy. Loads of women, when they talk about fantasies go, 'My fantasy would be a sailor,' and I'm like, 'No, really, what do you actually masturbate over the most?' and they're like, 'Memory sex.' It's the remembering of a moment.

I feel pretty relaxed about my sexuality. My body image is quite different; it's *really* irritating, it's so annoying. The one time when a woman doesn't feel self-conscious about her body is in the midst of an orgasm. She's not holding onto herself. When I'm in the middle of an orgasm, I'm not going, 'Does my bum look big in this?' I'm like, 'Whoo-whoo-hoo!' and I'm pulling not great faces. I don't care! I'm in the space of complete oneness and it might be gone within seconds but usually a female orgasm allows itself to be an extended orgasm. An orgasm spreads up around my whole body so my hand is not excluded, or my foot, or my knees so I have a whole-body experience. It lasts hours because I'm still having sensa-tions and I let them come. It's like the sea; you can't really say how long the wave lasted. Because it's all connected. The waves keep coming in. It's like asking the sea, 'How big are you?'

I genuinely think there's sweet delight, sweet innocence, wonderful, fiery, animal delight in sex and sexuality. Even dipping my toe into cold water – I have to say water because that's my thing – can satisfy me. Nature has such variety – *she* has such variety – that I'll never be bored and I can get my needs met really fast because I could go outside now and go, 'Ah!' and sit in the sun. Or if it's raining I can have a different sensation. But you couldn't say to a lover, 'Could you blow warm air over my skin for an hour?' The sun and wind will do that for me. Nature gives us so many things.'

# 17

# Victorian

Victoria, 33, Bristol

*'Maybe in an average session six or eight orgasms'*

'From the age of eleven onwards if I was watching a television programme and the hero was incapacitated – if he was a warrior and he was wounded and needed to be cared for – the vulnerability that I saw in that man was probably my first stirrings of 'Oh, what's this?' and I felt a physical sensation of longing and a sense of wanting to connect with that person. The only way I can find myself feeling sexual is to imagine I am nursing some man who is hurt. I might be fantasising about my partner – I feel embarrassed to say it – and his knee hurts and so he's lying there in our flat and I'm looking after him. But then the fantasy becomes him breaking his leg or having a stroke and I'm like, 'No! No! No! Get out of my head! That is not what I want to happen.' I don't want someone to suffer so I can have pleasure. Where is the line between that and sadism? I don't want him to be in pain so I try to, I police my own thoughts. I'm kind of, 'That's an acceptable thought, that's not an acceptable thought,' so there's never an abandonment through fantasy.

I remember being drunk and confessing to my brother that this was my fantasy and he said, 'Well, the men can't run away.' I thought, 'That's very insightful – the git!' He cut right to the quick. I need them to need me. I am critical of myself for having this fantasy, yet I can't be alone – that nursey role is incredibly common in popular culture because I see it everywhere. If I watch a TV drama at some point the hero gets blown up or hurt or has a breakdown and he's vulnerable and there is always a woman there who is strong for him. So I can't be alone.

I had an experience when I was very young, my parents left me and my friend with a male babysitter who was only sixteen himself and he took advantage of that situation. He was touching us on the sofa and he was touching himself. It wasn't like I was systematically sodomised by an uncle. It was quite tame really. I was kind of absent during the experience; I was in my head, I was thinking, 'He'll stop in a minute.' I just lay there with a big resentment at my parents that I couldn't get hold of them – this was before mobile phones – because they had gone out to have a jolly old night and left me in that situation. It wasn't that it traumatised me at that time. It wasn't that it was a sexual thing, but strangely over the years my sexuality was never ... The metaphor of a bud that never opened.

For years in therapy I would start by saying, 'At seven, this thing happened with the babysitter,' thinking that was the beginning of it, but I don't know if that's realistic. I wonder if I picked up on it even younger. My parents were pregnant as young teenagers and the baby was born, lived, then died.

They then went out, drank, took drugs and went crazy and didn't have me until fifteen years later. They painted a picture of being from that liberal sixties generation but actually the messages I got were relentlessly prudish. We never talked about sex. I was always chastised for running around naked as a child, you know – 'Put some clothes on.' I really, really don't want to blame my parents. I think it goes back ancestrally. I do feel influenced by my Catholic heritage and strong Catholic ancestry, which my parents broke from but that sense of guilt and shame doesn't disappear in one generation.

I was starting to look womanly and get breasts at the age of nine or ten. I went to an all-girls' private school and there was this very dynamic power crowd, some of them more sexual and ladylike than others. I certainly was not in the pretty crowd. I remember being twelve when the rumours started about 'Did you know that so-and-so slept with so-and-so and did you know that so-and-so gave so-and-so a blow job?' Very quickly I formed this idea that everybody was out there doing sexual things and I was left behind. I remember crying and crying and my parents asking me what was wrong and me saying, 'I haven't got a boyfriend.' They must have thought, 'Gosh, she's twelve, what's she up to?' And so I did get a boyfriend. I went to one of those discos where everyone's lined up either side and I was matched up with a chubby lad and everyone said how sweet it was that the chubby ones found each other. We were at the exploring stage and we used to go and kiss in the wood and once he and I were in the bathroom and he locked the door and he got his willy out and I started to touch it and do you know, I haven't really progressed from that point in my life, when I was twelve where my sexuality stopped!

By the time I was eighteen years of age, I was eighteen stone. It was a catch-22: I didn't want to have sex because I was so overweight but I was so overweight probably because I didn't want to have sex. It was a protective thing. Because I went to an all-girls' school I had this idea that boys were different from girls and that we were separate. Then I was faced with going to university. I always thought I was going to be a nun and I was very frightened. On Freshers' Day I got myself really dolled up and I got myself a taxi into Leeds and I got out of the taxi and this group of lads went, 'Oi, Vanessa Feltz!' – Vanessa Feltz is the TV presenter who is very large – and I got back in the taxi and went home again. I felt so vulnerable and so keenly aware of being fat and being a target, and I felt very, very frightened.

I left university at twenty-three and time and time again I attracted weird people. I found myself drunk in alleys after nightclubs, and in strange men's beds. I lived in France for a year and when I went to scrap my car, this French guy I knew said he would drive me back and he stopped the car, locked the doors and asked for sex. I was always finding myself with creepy men in difficult situations and, as somebody who is very self-aware, I look back and realise I was sending out some strange signals: those men were culpable but there was something about me that was vulnerable, that was needy. The more those things happened the more frightened I got. I ended up in a cold, nothing kind of place.

I haven't had a lot of sex: I've had two boyfriends. The first one was very controlling about when I could see him. I'd go to his house on a Saturday night, we would watch TV and have dinner and then in the morning it would be sex, but I have perfected the blowjob. Through those difficult situations when men were pressurising me to have sex, the only way I could get out of that, I felt, was to offer a really fine blowjob, wait until they fell asleep, and get out! Once you've offered a man that, they don't really want to go through the rigmarole of turning you on and then having sex. Then occasionally we would have sex and it would be very painful, very forced. I remember him saying to the therapist when we did couple therapy, 'I don't want to have sex with somebody that I'm hurting. It doesn't turn me on to hurt her: er, er, no, stop, ouch!' There was nothing spontaneous, loose or peaceful about the situation at all.

I am in a relationship now. It doesn't really work sexually. A couple of weeks after I first met my partner, I went to stay with him at his flat and I seduced him. I made sure I was hair-free and put my fake tan on and I bought condoms and I was all prepared and he was a little bit blindsided by it, but we had sex on his living-room floor. And for the first time in my life somebody actually gave me oral sex. I was spreadeagled on the floor. And I was *mortified;* I was *absolutely mortified* that he would do that. I was like, '*Don't* go down *there!* Oh my God! You've no idea what you're doing. Stop it!' From that, he did bring me to orgasm and then we started the rigmarole of penetration and I froze up. I said to him, 'This is so painful. But this is normal – I'm like this all the time.' He was on top and he said, 'Do you feel you're a bit trapped with me being on top?' and I said, 'I do a bit,' and he said, 'I'll go on my back and you go on top.'

So I'm sitting on top of him but still gravity doesn't help. I can be sitting on top of an erect penis and not let go. It was such a ludicrous situation that I made a light-hearted joke about it and he laughed and I started to laugh and the more I laughed the more I slid down and so I was being penetrated. He said to me, 'You're not supposed to laugh during sex.' That made me laugh even more and so we were entwined and he was inside me and we were laughing, and he said, 'This was obviously what it was meant to be; don't give yourself a hard time about it.' So that was the end of it. I wouldn't say we went on to have sex. I actually really enjoyed giving him a blowjob because he'd earned it! It was such a liberating experience. That was the first time.

Then there have been a couple more times when we've had sex and it has always been difficult and always forced and it didn't flow. And I do think that guys are as sensitive as I am – he's sensitive, I'm sensitive – and men find it hard and think, 'You didn't find me attractive enough.' The self-worth thing comes in. We had sex again on his birthday, though it wasn't full penetrative sex; it was oral sex and cuddling. We had a go at penetration. That was in the summer, eight months ago now. I haven't really slept with my partner since. I still feel hopeful that he and I will go there again, I don't want it to be a deal-breaker because I don't want to go into what I haven't got, when I've got someone who's so lovely and loving. A lot of women would kill to have somebody who loves them and understands them and can hug them and have a soul connection with them: it's really profound.

I am very blessed, considering my experiences and preferences, to have found somebody who doesn't have a sex drive, who doesn't want to force it on me. Well, I think he does have a sex drive. I have a private masturbation relationship with myself, and he seems to as well. We're cuddly, we're tactile, we love each other, but we don't have sex, we don't share a bed. He's very pragmatic, he always says to me, 'Take it a day at a time. There's no reason to look at what we've got today and think, this isn't good enough.' And I'm very grateful to have the relationship I've got. It's very serene, we enjoy each other's company and we're both spiritual people, we pray and meditate together, we talk about things, we laugh a lot, we really laugh like crazy people sometimes. He has a way of making me laugh: no one's really ever tickled me like that. It's not a problem for me, not unless I make it one. I could make it a problem because I want to be socially acceptable.

When I've had sex I've not felt any pleasure. None whatsoever. It's very, very painful. So I shut. I clam up. Penetration is painful. But also orgasm. When I orgasm I get cramps like period cramps that stay with me and this has been investigated at length by medical types and I've been told I've got a clean bill of health. I've never been penetrated and had an orgasm at the same time so I don't know what it feels like to orgasm with something meeting the waves of contractions. My orgasm's never met resistance, which I imagine must be quite pleasurable.

When I masturbate I have many, many orgasms. Loads! It's known to have gone on for hours. Maybe, in an average session, six or eight orgasms. The first orgasm is the best, then they taper off – they might just be mini ones at the end but by then I'm past the point of it being pleasurable. I equate masturbation with my eating disorders. It's not fun to eat until you're sick, but I did that. It feels good at the first mouthful and I think, 'Oh, this feels nice,' and the second sensation feels good, then I tip over to the point where I've had too much and I'm chasing that pleasure into the chasm. It's not satisfying. But if I stop after the first orgasm I'm unsatisfied. It's physically empty but also emotionally and spiritually empty. I masturbate until I'm absolutely spent and I always end up crying myself to sleep. It's not a release: it's a tragedy. Masturbation feels unfulfilling and pointless because it's so empty. It physically hurts and that's when the cramps start and then I have to curl up. I don't think of physical pain as being separate from emotional and spiritual pain, I tend to feel everything emotionally.

Because I've never enjoyed sex I don't think I'm trying to recapture something. It's a fire that's not been kindled yet. I don't particularly want to kindle it. I could function perfectly well for the rest of my life without exploring sex. I'm thirty-three and intellectually I want to enjoy sex and be sexual but I don't feel it in any deeper sense. I have an incredibly passionate, loving life, I'm somebody who goes out and I give a lot of love and get a lot of love. I feel so validated by the love that I receive that I don't feel less for not being a particularly sexual person.

I wouldn't share my fantasies. Even though I don't think they're the worst things in the world I still feel shame about them. Perhaps I've got the personality of a Victorian lady. I feel like I'm from another era and don't belong in this world. Sometimes I feel like a child at a very busy junction thinking, 'Gosh, this world is so crazy, it's so mad,' so that I feel like I belong to another time and place. I find the realities of life all very yucky so I tend to prefer to be in a light space of love and peace. Yet I know I'm not fulfilled spiritually if I'm avoidant of my human side. I know that. We're spiritual beings having human experiences, but I don't want to go and live in a cave in the Himalayas and meditate and achieve enlightenment. I want to fully inhabit my body and to be at one with the experience of being human. My journey is about learning to be me – who I actually am, in this body, in this life. To fully experience the body I have. To find a way of being comfortable with my sexuality, which is dormant or yet to be awakened, I suppose.

It's been a revelation thinking about this. I hear talk – I've heard rumours – that sex can be incredibly spiritual. I've heard that people merge at the point of orgasm, that there's a sense of being lost in that, completely abandoned, complete surrender. If I experienced that once in my life then I would be sexually satisfied.'

# 18

# Guide leader

Hilary, 68, Sheffield

*'I have a six-foot-three handsome Yorkshire
man; you know what I mean?'*

'I bloom where I'm planted! I'm still in the Girl Guide movement – well, I was a Brownie! I loved being in the Brownies. I passed all the badges, got the wings and flew to the Girl Guides. Years later, I was home in Sheffield and they said, 'Oh, Hilary, would you help with the Girl Guides?' and I said, 'Well ...' And they said, 'It's only two hours a week.' I did go and I've thoroughly enjoyed it ever since and I've done thirty years. Absolutely fabulous.

I was the youngest of eleven children. Happy family. My father's family came from Dublin during the potato famine to work in the factories. My mother was born in 1899. My mum was wonderful. I went to an old-fashioned, all-girls' convent school with the nuns teaching us. I was at the Immaculate Conception School – the name itself! Every excuse in the world, isn't it? I'm a

Christian. I questioned it, but I believe. My faith has affected my sexuality. Oh, absolutely! Guilt, guilt, guilt. Catholics generally have this guilt thing. I mean, oh, for goodness sake, we didn't talk about sex at all growing up. I never heard the word *sex* mentioned at home. My mother had eleven children and I used to think, 'When did I ever see you in bed?' I never saw her in bed, not until she was ill because she was always up before everyone and she would never go to bed until everyone was home. I was born in the bed in the bedroom. I was born four pound with the yellow jaundice and they didn't think I was going to live, but I was very tenacious and I wouldn't die! I bloom where I'm planted. I said, 'I bet you really didn't want me, because with ten children you wouldn't have wanted eleven.' Forty-six when she had me. She said, 'Every baby comes for a reason,' and my reason was because – it was a long time afterwards – I was the one that looked after her. Amazing, eh?

I met my husband. He is Catholic now, although he wasn't Catholic when we met. I didn't go to pubs but this friend said, 'Oh God, come on, Hilary, let's go to the pubs,' so we went to this pub and there was this group on and it was really nice, and my husband was there. We actually saw each other over a crowded room, I looked and he looked and our eyes met, and we just knew there was something. And that was it. Amazing! I was twenty-one when I got married. When we were married, you didn't have sex before you were married, supposedly. You didn't – except that you get very near to it! You just try it to see if it can work, and then you know if it can work on a sexual level. But officially, no. But you have to make sure, to try. It was when the pill had just come out so I thought, 'Oh, I'll go on the pill' just before, *just* before, only just before, we got married. I didn't really have sex all the time before I was married, other than to try it!

165

I went on the pill and it was good really. After a while, I got a conscience about the pill and I decided I wouldn't go on it. But then it was this horrible trauma because we went to the rhythm method where you can only have sex on a certain day and I'd think, 'Oh, my temperature!' I had a thermometer stuck up my bum. Then the nurse said, 'Try it under your arm.' But under your arm isn't as accurate as ... you know. I had that thermometer everywhere! A different one in my mouth! Then I'd have to record my temperature every day on this chart to see if it was going up or down and then, 'Ah! Today's the day, we can have sex today!' And I'd say to Geoffrey, 'This is the day!' He'd be all of a dither. And so this was the day. Oh, but it was wearing. I was that bothered about this flipping temperature thing – this was to avoid having children, which is probably against all our principles anyway! Then we got really quite fed up with that. And we thought we'd go for a baby.

We had a protected environment when we were being brought up. My husband is proper Yorkshire and he has a dry sense of humour. You see, he's quite a wit and he'd have a laugh. I'd be out with Geoffrey and there would be all these jokes that I wouldn't understand and Geoffrey would say, 'I'll tell you when we're in bed tonight. Just laugh.' I've only seen one DVD that was raunchy, which somebody gave me! I was in my late forties. And it was quite funny; it was '*Eeh!*' I don't like things like that really. No, I'm more of a sweetie. Sex education was just ourselves learning and developing ourselves. We think maybe we should have got books and read about different things but we didn't. There are things I would do, oral and all the rest of it. Yes. So we've played around but haven't done anything planned, or said, 'Let's look at this book and do it this way.' But maybe we should. Maybe that's our fiftieth anniversary treat. Once we were out in the country, because we're walkers. We lay on the grass and when it happens, it's magical, isn't it? I don't think sex as a routine is a brilliant thing. It should be something you feel and you want and you are. For me, that kind of love is tenderness and nice. It's erotic at times as well. Makes me feel good. It's sensual and all those things that give us elation and that's really, really good.

Recently my husband has had cancer and we've just had word that it looks clear, although it's not totally finished with. It has affected him; he hasn't been able to enjoy the physical ... to rise to the occasion! But as you get older and more understanding you get a deeper love as well. You go up and down through things, don't you? And I've thought, 'I'm this that and the other and you're not,' and then I realise, 'Well, no, I'm not really, and you are.' Then all of a sudden it's like the first meeting and I really want to be with him and I thought, 'Gosh! This is turning a whole circle. Definitely. The love. It's as if I've come back to the beginning. He wants to be with me, yes, yes,' and I think, 'Yes.' It's almost as if it's new. He's seventy-five and he's missing me as he would at the very beginning. The love has deepened, if you can imagine it. Somehow he's got more beautiful; the marriage has got more beautiful. Can you believe it? You can't really imagine it because I thought the young bits and the new bits are the most beautiful, but now it's a deeper love and trust. It can happen, that, you know.

We've been married since 1967. And we always celebrate wedding anniversaries. Would you believe, for our twenty-fifth wedding anniversary the Girl Guides brought the Guide tent and we pretended it was a marquee. We put it up in the garden and my friends decorated it pink. And we had a roasting pig and caterers, and we all got dressed up in black tie and it was a fabulous party. Then for our fortieth wedding anniversary we said, 'Shall we go on a cruise?' But we thought everybody can enjoy a party so we had a party in the village hall and everybody was imagining we were going to have this roasting pig. So we thought we'd better get one, so we did. It was once in a lifetime. I got this ruby dress – fabulous dress – and it was all sequins and fitted but it was stunning. And we said to everybody to come in the colour ruby. And it was wonderful. Super. Super-duper. It was really a super do.

I definitely still have a libido and I always have, it's only that my husband has a bit less now, because he's been so poorly. Sometimes I miss sex. Oh yes. I actually, in some situations, believe in – well, I wouldn't call it prostitution. If a marriage doesn't have sex and one person wants sex why is it wrong for them to go somewhere else? But not have a relationship. I mean, you wouldn't think I'd think it and I probably shouldn't as a Catholic, but it's serving their need, isn't it? I was thinking of it, but I can't fancy anybody. I couldn't just go and have sex with a dirty old man. I'd have to have a really nice-looking escort! My husband wouldn't like it. But then again, I've never asked him! He'd just be very embarrassed and hurt because *he* couldn't do it. I don't have my own private fantasies. Well, sometimes I think, oh, I could really fancy somebody – my husband – touching my body and I'm turned on and my libido's working. But I don't wish I could hang on a tree and be doing whatever. Maybe I'm not touching the right buttons on myself.

It doesn't bother me that I've never slept with anyone else. I don't think of it in that way. I never particularly fancied anyone else. But then again I have a six-foot-three, handsome Yorkshire man; you know what I mean? He's rugged and he's very straightforward – what you see is what you get. Well, somebody else might say he was ugly, but he's generally pleasing to people. Other people could be attracted to him. Now I'm much more aware. Now I don't put myself or Geoffrey into a position where it could lead to something with someone else. Because there's some wicked women out there, especially schoolteachers.

Now that I've retired from my career in NatWest bank, I also support a national charity against child exploitation. I've recently been made an ambassador for the charity and went to the United Nations with them. One, I raise awareness. Two, I raise money by having a ladies' lunch. At the last count, they had thirty-something exploited children in Sheffield, from age eleven to twenty. The exploited children are very lonely people and they want to be loved. And these men who groom them can identify them. Why the pimps are doing it is a difficult one. The paedophiles, without a doubt, have an addiction to sex and they can't help themselves: they see it and want it and have to have it. Others are definitely money-making. You can make a fortune. It's a different trade and industry – anything for money. Would you sell your child? No. But someone else might.

The girls are like sex machines. Words couldn't express what I see. I feel compassion for them and I can't help but support the children, even if it's to sew toilet bags. When I go to the supermarket I *Buy One Get One Free* and I put the free one in the toilet bag. I put in a toothbrush, soap, facecloth; things like that. One day a week the charity opens their centre and exploited children can drop in off the street. The charity lets them have a hot meal and a shower and gives them one of these new toilet bags, and the toilet bags work superbly well, because nobody wants to use somebody else's soap after them, and the girls can take them away as well. Every little helps.

I've been thinking about my friends' daughters and I

thought, what do I call them: loose women? I think women are too promiscuous now. Sometimes people too readily have sex, like going to the toilet. Some people give up too soon, and think, 'Well, I'm not standing this any more; I'm leaving, because of der, der, der.' I can leave and I could have and I don't, probably because I'm Catholic. When I visited my Auntie Phoebe in the retirement home, I said to her something negative about my husband and she looked at me – she was ninety-four – and she said, 'So-and-so, her husband was at the council meetings and here, there and everywhere and she just had to put up with it. Hilary, can't you just put up with it?' And I thought, of course I could just put up with it and get on. But then it comes back again. You get over it. And I mean, who's perfect? And to be perfect all the time, you'd be pretty boring, wouldn't you? And we've stood the test of time.

And sex is for a long-term relationship, for its development, for the blossoming, blooming, flowering, coming to the fore. That is what I feel sex is for. Well, it is a sacrament; it's the sacrament of sex, really, isn't it? Marriage is a sacrament when you are having sex. In the Catholic faith they say marriage is for the procreation of children. It isn't, surely, because I wouldn't be married because I haven't got children – which can you believe after that thermometer! Just can't understand, can you? But anyway, there you are. We're parents to hundreds of others. My husband was a deputy head of a comprehensive school and someone said to my husband, 'Have you any kids?' and he said, 'I've got none of my own but I've got every bugger else's!'

Organisms – oh yeah! That's the culmination of everything. Yeah, it is. I do think that. Yes, I do have organisms; I mean orgasms. Perhaps I'm very fortunate: in an unplanned and unknown way I've experienced so much of my body, and our bodies, which has developed into experiencing all these lovely things. There's the tenderness and the excitement and the organisms and then we maybe want to do it again. I've been very fortunate. All I say is bloom where you stand, be as good as you can wherever you are, in whatever moment. And then you can look back later and you don't realise how fortunate you've been and what you've done. You've got to be the best you can whenever you can in that moment.'

# 19

# Beauty contestant

Ariel, 35, Reading

*'Why shouldn't fat women have as much sex as everybody else?'*

'I've entered a beauty competition – it's for plus-size women. The finals are in two weeks in Birmingham. For the swimwear round, I've covered a bra and knickers in bright green Lycra and sparkly purple netting to make a Little Mermaid outfit. Rather than just turning up in a swimsuit, I thought I'd turn up with my hair Ariel-fied and Ariel outfit on. It's because of Ariel in *The Little Mermaid*, and because my hair is red. I'm going to get a bubble gun and use it when I get to the end of the runway. God knows how I'm going to do it. I'm not embarrassed, but I'm not a flaunty, get-it-all-out kind: I feel self-conscious in a bikini. I think most women do.

The plus-size beauty pageant is size 18 or over. I don't know if I'm in with a chance. I'm a UK size 26. In stones – it's too much! Over twenty. There is an acceptable plus-size shape when it comes to modelling which is a slim face and an hourglass figure, but slightly bigger, size 20 plus: bigger bust, smaller waist, bigger hips. You very rarely see the likes of someone with my body shape – I've got a fat chin, my belly is bigger than my boobs, my hips aren't that big. I've not got the right shape for fashion – a lot of girls in the competition have – so I think they'll win over me.

I go to this club night in London called For Big Girls. It's a plus-size acceptance night for girls and guys who are bigger and girls/guys who like bigger, to go and have a nice night out without all that ... You can wear what you like, you can dance how you like, you can be who you are without anyone going, 'Urgh, look at her! She's so fat! Oh my God – what is she wearing? Oh my God, she shouldn't wear that. She's too fat to wear that.' All those things you might hear in a mainstream bar. I've been in a group of women and someone will go, 'Oh my God, did you see the size of her arse in that?' I just think, 'So what? Her arse is the size of her arse! What's it got to do with you? How does that affect her personality? It doesn't affect if she's a nice person or not, does it?' Women are very judgmental of other women – I'm so generalising here – If I go out, I would worry about what the women would say more than the men.

I saw the pageant in previous years with a couple of friends from the club night and they said, 'Why don't you enter?' and I thought, 'No, no, I can't do that.' Then I just thought, 'All right then, I will.' So I went to model training camp to learn how to walk which, after thirty-five years, I thought I was pretty good at. I wasn't, it turns out! It was model walking. And media training; how to speak to the media, how to deal with negative press – because that will happen. Anyone who gets through to being the winner will get negative press.

For a lot of people there, that is their only social night out because unfortunately people are very mean, society is very mean. Saying something negative about someone because they're fat is the last form of discrimination that is completely acceptable in society, and legal. It's also the last discrimination that's humorous. If you watch any stand-up comedians, it's always fat jokes and it's hilarious. If someone falls over and they're fat, it's funnier than someone skinnier falling over because, 'Oh, they're fat.' There's a whole fat-shaming society at the moment.

Some men like big women. Definitely. You've got men who fantasise about having sex with fat women. Or they have this desire to make women fatter; men who like to feed women to make them fatter. That's more of a fetish. I think a lot of men like curvy women, because they want her to have bits on her that are female! Boobs and bum and hips. Men like fat women. It's common. When I was younger, being bigger stopped me getting a boyfriend. Because younger men are more interested in what their mates think. One of my friends had it happen to her: she had a boyfriend for a couple of months but never met his friends, never met his family, never met anybody. It turned out he really liked her, he wanted to be with her, but he was too embarrassed because she was fat. That happens *a lot* when people are younger. When I was younger I would never go out with men who said they liked fat girls because I thought they were weirdos because I had no body acceptance.

There's not a shortage of people out there that I could go on a date with now. Most of the pressure is from ourselves and other women. Men care less than we think they do. Most men would go, 'Oh, all right then,' if sex was offered to them. They probably wouldn't care. A year ago when I was walking to work – I work in IT – this guy was looking across the road at me, and I thought, what's he looking at, why is he staring? He came up to me and he said, 'I just want to tell you that you're looking really nice today. Have a really nice day.' You don't expect that, walking down the street.

I've always said, I don't meet men and then end up in bed with them and they expect underneath all my clothes I'm a size 8. They must know that I'm fat before I take my clothes off! There's no point hiding in the dark under the bedsheets so they don't see my fat bits, because what's the point? Because they know that I'm fat and if they didn't like it before, they're not going to like it now.

One of my friends has got a boyfriend and she's very much, 'Lights off, get under the covers, don't squeeze my fat bits.' Surely if he's having sex with you, he likes you? He probably *wants* to do that, he probably wants to turn the lights on. Women are too hung up when they are in bed with someone about what they look like, because I don't think men care. If you're in a relationship with someone long-term, I don't think that your partner is going to care.

My weight doesn't affect how I have sex. I go on top. Yeah. Men like that – that's a power thing. In respect of the ergonomics of it and position-wise, I might have to move in slightly different ways. Maybe I can't get into a certain position because I can't get my legs over my head because my tummy's in the way – things like that. I'll try it. I'll try and get in that position but I can't guarantee my flexibility is that good. Depends what size your partner is. But I'm willing!

My sexual fantasies are normal things. Sex outside: I suppose it's because you could get seen by people. Sex in nature – in fields rather than in the high street. I thought about being with girls in fantasies – I don't think that's anything that 90 per cent of women haven't thought about. Sex in a hot tub, which I did; that was fine. I've got a hot tub, it's a blow-up one, it's really good. It's like a proper hot tub and you pump it up. It's for outside. I had a gazebo over the top of it. If the neighbours are looking, that's their problem! Shouldn't be looking, should they, in my garden if they don't want to see things like that.

I don't think a lot of people act on their sexual fantasies because I don't think they are ever as good as you think they are going to be. I mean, sex in a hot tub is great but as a woman, sex in water is not that comfortable. It ends up being quite painful and you go, 'Oh, this isn't quite what I thought it would be. Oh well. Done it now. Ticked that off my list.' The whole concept of sex is just odd. If you actually think about what we do during sex, it's weird, isn't it?

I've got a couple of Ann Summers outfits. Got a little policewoman set. It's got a tutu-y skirt to it. For role playing. The other person would be a prisoner. Never got to the role-playing bit, never get that far, just ends up outfit and fun. Not a very good policewoman. Rubbish! I've got a French maid's outfit, which is see-through. No cleaning. It's a bit of fun, isn't it? Just go off and get changed and come back in an outfit. Ta da! Surprising him when he's watching *Top Gear* on telly. 'Oh! Oh, hello. All right then.' Good fun really. With anything to do with sex, it's got to be fun. And don't hold back; there's no point if you've got that far with someone.

My weight is flexible. I do eat three meals a day. Yeah, I have my vices, I have a Chinese takeaway here and there, I have this, that and the other and what I want. If there's something to do with my health that needs attention and I needed to lose weight, then I'd lose weight. There are so many other things that you are as a woman as opposed to your flesh and the size of it. It's just packaging, isn't it, at the end of the day? I've tried to starve myself, I've tried to make myself sick, but it was a vicious circle of self-hatred and being eternally depressed with my life and myself. In my late twenties I got fed up with berating myself for not being perfect. I just thought, 'Why am I doing this to myself? Why don't I either go and lose weight or accept myself as I am and get on with my life, because there's no point stopping myself from doing things.' I'm quite attached to my body and, as much as I probably could lose a few pounds here and there, if I want to I will, if I don't want to, I won't. My weight is just one part of my life. I don't see it – pardon the pun! – as a big part of my life.

There's still much more pressure to look a certain way, common to society's views of what is attractive and sexual and beautiful. Paintings in the eighteenth century were always of women who were larger. A lot of painters apparently – I watched a programme on it – prefer to paint bigger women because there's more fluidity. There's more to draw, I suppose. It's more challenging and interesting.

Being fat is much more of a female issue than it is a male issue. Some people see someone who's fat as very non-sexual, as in, 'Fat people shouldn't have sex.' That fat people should hide themselves away. I don't follow that rule! I don't follow that way of thinking at all. I'm just like everyone else – why not? Why shouldn't fat women have as much sex as everybody else? It's never been something that's stopped me. I don't think you have to be thin to be sexy. I can tell you a hundred men who disagree with that. A fat woman can be sexy. Of course she can. Sexy is not about your perception of yourself necessarily, it's about someone else's perception of you. Attractiveness is individual. I might find a six-foot-two rugby player attractive, you may not.

The girls I've been hanging around with over the last couple of years promote body confidence and that has made me better at accepting myself. On stage in the beauty pageant, I just think, 'I'm here, that's it.' And I enjoy myself as a woman. I like to make an effort with how I look. I have days when I think I look shit; everyone does. But mostly I love the clothes I wear. I'm really into skater dresses. And leggings and boots. I don't try and hide. I dress how I like to dress and how I think looks good. When I go to club nights, I wear a black corset and tutu; that's really cool. I went to a music festival recently and I wore that outfit, which was fun. I look in the mirror and think, 'Oh, yeah, I'm hot to trot!'

I've always wanted bigger boobs. Men like them. I often see myself with bigger boobs. More like a mermaid! Really shapely. All men like mermaids. Mermaids sing and lure men in with their songs: that's the myth. And mermaids get what they want. I'll come back as a mermaid.'

# 20

# Pianist

Farah, 20, London

*'I'm not cheating on him but ...'*

'I've got a boyfriend. I've been in a bit of a funny situation in the last few months: I've been re-evaluating my relationship. He's a couple of years older than me, so roughly my age. Fairly tall, skinny. Kind of got long blond hair down to the neck. He was in the year above me at uni doing music as well. I like him, yeah. Not that I'm going to do anything with anyone else. He's a cuddly person and I thought I was, but he's definitely very cuddly! I'm not blaming my boyfriend but it's like a barrier between cuddly and sexual. Whenever we talk about our relationship in a sexual way we end up arguing and it doesn't go anywhere. There's something about the undertones that I don't like when he starts talking about women.

He doesn't understand. Foreplay. Lack of. And I'm not wanting to ask for it because I don't want to have to ask for it every time. Why doesn't he just know what I want? He pretty much wants to have penetrative sex. He doesn't mind me doing foreplay on him, and that's the annoying thing. Whenever I get annoyed with specific behaviours or things that he's said, he doesn't get why I get wound up. He just says, 'I said I'm sorry. I can't help it. That was me being stupid.' I'm like, 'Stop. Being. Stupid. And start getting it.' He seems not that experienced. We've worked in a certain way for two years and now I suppose I have to decide. I can't imagine that he would start doing foreplay. Maybe I'm just demanding. Maybe I was ready to commit before. But then I was, 'Hold on; this is the only guy I've had sex with. I can't imagine the rest of my life with only one person.'

I feel bad now. I feel so bad. Oh man! I'm not cheating on him but ... Well, yeah, I kind of know someone else. It's just a recent development and we had a one-off. I didn't fully sleep with him. We've been friends for the last year at uni. I don't know if I like him a lot. I know that sounds bad! There's always the thing if you want something you shouldn't have, it's going to escalate, so I'm trying to keep cool about it.

He's older, maybe in his forties. When he was younger he was a goth. He's always had a vampire persona kind of thing. Because of the goth thing I thought he would be into something kinky. Yeah, I was curious and excited to get to know him in another way. He says when he tells people, sometimes they step away because they find it weird or they don't like blood. I think that you bite or scratch until you bleed. I was like, 'I know the sex stuff you're into. Whatever. That's cool.' I knew if I asked him questions he would answer. So I asked the questions – and I knew that was going down a bad path. I texted him about the vampire thing. He told me what he did to his ex – like screaming, biting her. I texted back saying, 'I don't think I would scream.' That was a bit of a bold move.

We went to the pub and he was like, 'Okay, one drink.' He's told me he's autistic. Maybe that's why he thinks quite clearly about stuff. And I genuinely wasn't trying to offer him drinks but then we kept drinking and chatting. So we walked back and got outside his house – and I can't believe I even said it – I just said to him, really deadpan, 'So you're not going to invite me in, then?' and he was like, 'Okay.' I didn't even try to seduce him. It was like, 'Well, this is what you were texting about Saturday.' But when I got to his room it was really different from what I was expecting because I was expecting more of a dark theme, and it wasn't. It looked normal; it could be my room, with lots of books and CDs. I said, 'I can't be leaving here with bite marks, otherwise it's going to show!' He did bite me on my neck, but in a normal way. It hurt a little bit but not really. Yeah. I think what I had in my head was a bit exaggerated. I'd like to do the vampire stuff. I want to try so much sexually that I haven't tried before.

Oh God. This is where I start digging a hole for myself. My ex was older as well. This was the one before my boyfriend. He was in his fifties. I was seventeen. He was my piano teacher. It just kind of started. We would talk a lot about music and stuff and send a lot of emails. I knew of him for one year, and for the second year he was my piano teacher. It was a few months of just talking and beginning to feel stuff but not acting on it and not saying anything to him. It was May; it was the last term of school. We were chatting outside the lessons so, because that was happening, I asked him upfront whether he had feelings for me and then, yeah, we started meeting outside of the lessons. That was nice. I wasn't happy doing my A Levels and I don't think he was that happy doing his job. I was cross with my dad just in general but that's another story, so it was probably as a bit of escapism for both of us. I think I was in love with him. Yeah. He was in love with me. The age difference mattered because I knew other people were going to judge and criticise, but for us it didn't seem to matter.

Once I went really early in the morning to his house, the earliest I could get there, before five. That was the one time I actually got into bed with him – because I was exhausted. I didn't sleep the night before so I fell asleep, which was nice. It wasn't even staying overnight in a sexual way; it was cuddling up to him in bed. I wasn't really sexually scared; maybe there were a lot of nerves from both of us. He wasn't married. He hadn't slept with other students, it was just me. I liked him, and he liked me. I didn't sleep with him, not properly. We decided not to sleep together. Because if anything happened and it came out – which it did – then it would make it worse. I was waiting to finish school and then I was going to be open about it – or I was going to try.

It was a secret. It all came out in the end. My dad looked at my phone so, yeah … chaos happened. I'm being so melodramatic here! My dad was going ape-shit. My mum said nothing. She knew. I haven't talked to her about it. My mum was away in Iran for a couple of weeks. I wasn't going to talk to anyone. I mean, I didn't even know where to start. My dad contacted my school and it was a nightmare. The piano teacher got sacked, there were police investigations and all sorts of crazy stuff. I don't know what happened to him, but probably he won't be able to get a job now. It ended abruptly, very much so. I had no contact with him because I wasn't allowed to and then I was starting uni so I thought, 'I need to move on.' So I didn't contact him again and that was it, really. He was upset – yeah.

When it ended, I did fantasise because I missed the piano teacher. I suppose you fantasise about what you can't have.

Maybe I'm imagining fantasies to be specific images. I latch more onto memories and feeling and touch. I don't really remember sexual fantasies. They just come into my mind and I forget about them because I don't think I'm going to live it out. When I was younger and on long car journeys I used to fantasise I was doing it in a field. Maybe that ties in with going away or abroad and imagining finding someone different there. That's an early teenage fantasy. I was fairly late having my first boyfriend. I was sixteen; everyone else had a boyfriend before that. I felt sexually ready to go but no one was there. I don't really fantasise now – now I'm having sex. The more I'm doing it the less I have to imagine it.

I ended up feeling so much more guilt over the piano teacher – although he was single and I was single. But now I feel like I'm doing something that's morally more wrong. No one would bat an eyelid because people cheat all the time and I'm no different, but I had to deal with a lot more guilt with my ex. It's really weird. I know that seeing the goth is worse and I should feel worse. I fantasise about sleeping with the goth. I want to see the goth guy again. I'm not planning to. It was a one-off but if it continues, it's just cheating. Maybe I'm not in two minds as much as I was because normally with affairs you're kind of, 'Oh, it just happened.' But this didn't, I was very decisive about it. I wanted to be sexual with the goth. In some ways I don't know who I like but if someone likes me I like them back.

I can't tell my boyfriend; he'd be heartbroken. I'm not scared of leaving my boyfriend. I'm more worried about him being hurt. It's weird because I had to spend some time with my boyfriend last night. It was the Music Final Degree Show. I don't know if he can sense anything, he's not that emotionally in tune with me – but he did ask because – well, I wasn't holding his hand. I did find it harder to look into his eyes. It's probably not good but ...

My family would be horrified. If my mum was as religious and strict as her family back in Iran none of this would have happened. My mum's Iranian and my dad's English. He's not religious, my mum is, though. She doesn't pray five times a day, she prays sometimes. She's probably prayed more in the last few years. I wouldn't necessarily call myself Muslim. I wasn't brought up a Muslim. My mum's a family therapist. She doesn't do family therapy on me. No, no, no, no, no! She's a really good mum. She's got many different cases dealing with families – well, no family is fully functional. She works with young people. She hasn't said, 'No sex before marriage,' but she's said, 'Go to uni first.' Which I did! I've done what she's told me to do and waited to get to uni before I had sex. Typical mum. She didn't even care about the marriage thing, she just wanted me to be older and not miss out on my education.

My mum wants to be open with me now because I have done things. Last Saturday night when I came back from the goth's house, I went to my mum's house and I was trying on some underwear and my mum walked in on me and I was like, 'Oh fuck,' and she was like, 'Sexy underwear!' She would never have said that before. But I felt bad. I put the underwear in my bag for the next day for when I was seeing the goth. Now my mum's accepting I'm sexual but she thinks I'm going to put the underwear on for my boyfriend so I feel really, really bad.

It's weird: I should consider my boyfriend now a normal relationship. At the start I was happy, I was like, I'm glad that I've found someone my own age; that's probably better. I don't know whether older guys are more experienced, or if that's something I think, or other people think? Both of the older men I've been with are different because they don't watch pornography. The piano teacher – he didn't watch porn. He told me. He was quite militant about it. He didn't like porn; he was more strongly against it. It's a different generation. The young men I know watch porn – definitely. My boyfriend's got expectations that are not the reality, like me being clean-shaven. He doesn't expect it, no, but he wants it. I don't mind that he wants it: but I don't get why. The way I look – what does it matter? He obviously wants oral sex before, like in porn the girls give the guy oral sex and then they have sex and it seems to always be in that order! And I end up living that out myself. I don't like oral sex as foreplay leading on to sex in a very predictable way. I think my boyfriend watches too much porn. Recently he's been stressed so he's watched it every day.

I found it unusual when I first went out with my boyfriend that he would have to watch porn to masturbate. I realised that's the norm now. I was like, 'Oh, okay.' Where he would go and watch porn, I would fantasise. Because when I'm fanta-sising I'm still trying to imagine it as if it's a real thing, the touch, even the smell, or the voice. I'm trying to imagine it as a whole. Obviously I'm by myself and it's not sex, but then porn is isolated towards that goal of getting an orgasm. It's not trying to encompass anything. The porn industry creates what they think men will like, what will get men there faster, but then everyone's affected by it, men and women. People are maybe more misinformed now because of porn. Porn can be very misinforming.

I'm feeling like I want more now. Maybe I'm just not happy. There's definitely a mental barrier between what you think you want, and the reality of it. I think you're always going to want what you can't have.'

## 21

# Nurse

Charlotte, 43, Manchester

*'I think vaginas are great'*

'I'm a senior staff nurse in an Early Pregnancy and Gynaecological Emergency Unit. And I've had some funny conversations about the fact that my job is looking up people's vaginas.
It feels *completely* normal to me to do that, but for a lot of people
that is like, '*Ow!* How can you look?' Most people, when I've said,
'Oh, yeah, I spend most of my time looking at vaginas,' will say,
'*Urgh!*' because vaginas are strong to look at. A lot of people
think it's a really unattractive place to look, particularly if
there's bleeding. Blood doesn't bother me either. I don't think
vaginas are disgusting at all. I think they're great. I think they
are actually beautiful. They are beautiful because a vagina is
how you can get a significant amount of pleasure from having
sex or doing whatever you want to do with yourself. It's also
where the baby comes out. It's creation. It's life. Life comes out
of there. And I think that's amazing.

Women don't generally think, 'My vagina is beautiful, it's great, it's amazing.' Most women are a bit embarrassed when they have an examination about how their vagina looks. It is private; it's called your 'privates'. It is a private place. I don't think it necessarily translates, though, that the fact that they feel embarrassed about a vaginal examination with a stranger when they're bleeding, with the associated potential anxiety and stress, that they also feel embarrassed with a partner or in a different setting.

I can appreciate a woman's body, but it's not remotely sexual for me. The thing about vaginas and the bits on the outside – the labia – is that they really vary in size and are very different. But the clitoris is pretty much the clitoris unless there's some sort of abnormality, which I don't see often. If you've had children the vagina can be a bit saggy, if you haven't had children it's much tighter. Then there's the cervix. The point of examining someone if they are bleeding in early pregnancy is to look at the cervix. With some people, examining and trying to see their cervix is nigh on impossible, and there are tricks of the trade.

When someone comes to see me for a vaginal examination I need to build up a rapport before I do an examination. Some women won't bat an eyelid and are like, 'Yeah, fine, whatever.' Some women will be really anxious. Some women will refuse. Sometimes I really need to do an examination and in that case, we might ask if they are happy to be sedated. I don't see genital mutilation that often but it's definitely there. There are levels of mutilation. It's absolutely horrendous. Sometimes it's cutting the clitoris off. Sometimes it's cutting the external genitalia and sometimes it is actually sewing up the vagina so there is only enough space for a dribble of wee and blood. But sometimes it's so bad that the blood doesn't come out and then the woman gets into a really bad way and has to have surgery, but that doesn't happen often. The people who carry it out in those countries are experienced and know the minimum size the hole can be. It is culturally acceptable in some areas and the women take the girls to have surgery, they're involved in it happening.

It took me – this is a bit embarrassing – ten years of being married to work out how to have a really great orgasm. That was because no one had told me. After two or three years of marriage I thought, 'There must be more than this.' I asked some girlfriends, 'How do you know if you're having an orgasm?' They said, 'Something happens in your head, it's a mind thing.' I was like, 'Oh, okay, I think that happens, so that's fine, I've had one of those.' Then *several years later* I was like, 'Err, cannot be right. There has to be more than this.' I asked some other girlfriends and they were all absolutely horrified! They said, 'No, it's *completely physical*.'

This was when I was a nurse. I was unusual in that I was so underexposed. I protected myself, but I was also very protected in the environment I grew up in, sexually. My upbringing was very straight-laced and I was really prudish. I always obeyed the rules, and the rules were that you didn't have sex before marriage. So how would I find out? Pornography is really fake and doesn't tell you anything. What would I do, read a book? What happens if someone saw me reading the book? And what book would I read anyway? Come to think of it, I did look at the *Kama Sutra* with David, my husband. Anyway, it didn't help me realise what I could be getting.

I don't remember having fantasies when I was younger. I remember as a little girl playing with myself, and when I was ten I had friends and we used to fiddle with each other. I thought that was quite nice but didn't have any idea of what

I was doing and I didn't do that for very long. The way that I managed to stick to the rules – i.e., not having sex before marriage – was really shutting myself down in that area. That's partly why it took me so long when we got married to feel free and easy about exploring it all.

Well, I became very good friends with a doctor who talks about masturbation, and anything like that, with no problems whatsoever – which I'm happy to now – but this was a few years ago. She said, 'You've got to work on it until you've had an orgasm and you'll certainly know when it happens: the waves, the feeling of it in the vagina. You need to play with yourself, you've got to get to know yourself,' which I hadn't ever done, hadn't occurred to me. So I started doing that. And I said to David, 'There's more than this; we've got to work it out.' He was great and he said, 'Okay, let's work it out.' And I learned how to give myself an orgasm and then he has joined in working it out and it's great now!

Now David and I pretend, we have role play, we do all sorts of things; we're quite creative. For example, I'm a secretary looking for a job. And he's my boss. And wants to have a good shag, basically. These days the children don't go to bed early so it's really difficult! So we meet for lunch on a Friday – well, we meet as employer and employee, have lunch and then have an afternoon shag. I would be the secretary and he would be the dodgy boss.

Personal trainer. I would be a personal trainer and he is someone who wants to get fit. I would dress up in my gym kit – my sexy gym kit – I don't really have any, but I would dress up in something. He would be in his work suit in the bedroom. We would stay in role for a bit but not very long. David bought me this hilarious bikini from Australia with a G-string and a triangle on the front. Oh my word. I've worn it for him, but not very often. I've also got this *little* pink skirt that he bought me. We've got a cleaner and she was sorting out our bedroom and she found it and said, 'Is this yours? Shall I give it to your daughter?' But it's obviously mine because it's big and I was like, 'Oh, I don't really wear it very often.'

It's usually David who comes out with the idea. I tried to. We went away for the weekend a couple of years ago and I decided to take the initiative for the scenario. It was a complete disaster because ... I don't know, it just didn't work. Looked around everywhere for some underwear and bought a negligée that didn't do it for him. It wasn't tight; it was a bit flowy, and because it was loose it wasn't flattering so that didn't help. Somehow the chemistry didn't work.

I like a scenario where I dress in something that makes me feel good. Yes. Enjoy that. I'm forty-three and I've really struggled with my weight over the years so I have times of feeling better about myself and I know when I feel happier about myself I'm more attractive to David. He's been absolutely brilliant and never commented about my weight but the whole thing is more enjoyable when I feel better about myself. A best scenario would be when I'm dressed up in something that makes me feel good, that is a bit naughty but not too naughty. I don't like it if it gets too ... I have an inbuilt line and I get to the point where I think, 'Okay, I want us to be normal now.' We haven't crossed that line but we've got close to it. I wouldn't like to be tied up; I wouldn't like anything that inflicted any pain. If there was something I didn't like I could quite happily say.

I quite like using a mirror when we're having sex. I've wondered about having somebody watching us or watching other people. I don't really mean that! I don't think I really do want that at all, actually. Very occasionally I glimpse it and then it's gone. I'd quite like to go for it outside; David doesn't like that at all. We did try once and it didn't work, because it was uncomfortable and we were potentially discovered! Occasionally we look at something erotic together. There's a fine line with that as well, sometimes it's okay and sometimes I don't really like it. I'm very, very fortunate that I'm in a marriage where we have a great relationship and when we can, we have good sex – not very often! – because there's a lack of opportunity and David hasn't got a massively high libido, which is fine. In fact, sometimes I'm like, 'Come on! For goodness sake.' I'd probably like to do it a bit more than we do. I think I'm quite satisfied actually.

The exposure from my work does really affect my view of sex and I think I would encourage my children not to, rather than go for it. To not have sex! I need to be careful what I say. For most women, it absolutely would not occur to them to say no to sex. A lot of women I've spoken to would feel uncomfortable saying no to their partners if they didn't want to have sex and would feel as though they needed to say 'yes' – I only say that from my observation. I've seen a lot of women in my time as a nurse and that is the impression that I've had. Because of my experiences at work with pregnancies, sexually transmitted diseases and the emotional trauma that comes from broken relationships, I think that to have a limited amount of sexual partners – or even none – until you find someone you will ideally marry for a long time is a great thing. Irrespective of my faith and my views, what I've observed, and the implications of having a child when you don't want a child, or having a termination are significant. You have either of those consequences with you for the rest of your life. But I don't really know how you can achieve no sexual partners without switching yourself off, like I did, and I don't think that's particularly brilliant. What makes me really sad is that people do just give it away so freely because it is so fragile and it's a precious thing. It's not a robust thing.

The thing about being a Christian is that I'm really working hard at the moment about what to say to the children. I don't want the children to repress themselves. They'd probably feel embarrassed and squeamish, me talking about sex to them, but I want to say to my daughter, 'Make sure you know how to get an orgasm', and to the boys, 'Make sure you know how to give your partner a really good orgasm.'

# 22

# Circus

Pandora, mid thirties, Kilburn, London

*'Sex brings out what's hidden'*

'Last night when I was on the trapeze and – you know, it's obviously very difficult and scary – there was a moment where I was supposed to come down and I ended up doing this really zappy thing. And everybody started laughing. And I *couldn't* stop laughing and I felt like I was having an orgasm. It was '*Yes!*' When I came off that trapeze – trust me – I was *full* of '*yes!*' Of sexiness. And I got into bed and I *could not* stop laughing. I felt really erotic, and not little. I felt really sensual and in my body from the inside out, so it wasn't a passive feeling. I see men look at me because I'm petite and go, 'Oh, she'll be sweet.' But I'm not; I'm quite a wild one.

Last night every woman who went up the trapeze, I could see who she was, maybe even sexually! One woman got on the trapeze and she was going, 'ow-ow-ow-ow-ha-ha-ha', and I thought she could be good fun! Another woman was really scared and she was going, 'Her-her-her-her'. I could see them expressing who they are and I imagined that is who they are within sex as well. On the final back flip I came down the wrong way. It was a funny moment but I really felt who I was in it. I had this moment of 'Wow!' Of being this raucous, outrageous woman really laughing. Everyone else was laughing really infectiously when I came down. I've had that from really good sex, when I get that moment where everything tumbles down, and all the things I thought and think – they're not really anything. It's a spiritual thing. Sex is a buster: it busts all your bullshit.

I come from an Irish Catholic background: very repressed. I need to say that. Sex is never talked about. My parents never had sex; we were all immaculate conceptions, which is something in itself, really. Immaculate Jesus came into my mum's body and she gave birth to me. So I knew nothing about sex apart from rats in the laboratories, which I got taught in the convent school I went to.

One of the things that I caught on to early on was – this is not anything that anyone taught me, I never read it in any books – when I got on a dance floor my body would express itself. I was very shy. I wasn't allowed boyfriends, and I was ambitious with my schoolwork, which I feel grateful for now. It all used to happen on dance floors, and then I'd get home and be a good girl. People thought I was very promiscuous, which I wasn't, I didn't have my first boyfriend until I was twenty. But something would just come out of my body. I remember this guy saying, 'God, you're so loose physically' – and I think he thought sexually as well. Feminists have written things about female rights but nobody talks about the fucking body, which is what sex *is*. It's as if women don't have a body other than what's projected on the screen and in pornography. There's something about dancing – it's the body. I don't think I was having sex on the dance floor; I was expressing all sorts of things. There's an energy in the body, and I really got that from dancing. Men often felt like, 'Whoa – what is that?' Even to this day: 'What is that woman?' and I think it's my sexual energy.

Recently there's one guy I do dance classes with. After I've been in the class with him, I get into bed and I'm like, I just want him! I'm not even up to thinking there's a relationship in it. He's almost a beautiful dancer but he's massively male. There's something really erotic about his skin. He's got a friend and I'm like, which one do I go for? Not that I'm going to. I fancy both of them in different ways, and it's definitely all physical. One has quite an emotional effect on me. I also feel it in my skin: he makes my skin feel like, 'Mmm.' I've imagined both of them being in bed with me and then they'd – you know – sleep with me together and then I'd pick one. Maybe I could have a harem of men.

One of the other guys at the dance class has a harem of women around him. All the women talk about it and they're not that pleased. One woman said, 'His cards are on the table; he's looking for a shag.' Every Friday night he goes to a bar and there are *loads* of women and more come there to meet him and he picks one – or two. Or three. The women are all quite sexy, they're beautiful dancers, they're all really in their bodies. I do have judgments and feelings about the harem thing. This friend was like, 'Yeah, it's really horrible and then he picks one and everyone thinks everything he says is really interesting.' And I think, 'Yeah, that is a bit shit.'

A lot of the young girls in the class are rushing around him. I'm glad I'm older because I think, 'I ain't doing that one with you.' I may not look like them, but I don't do that kind of thing. People think you should pitch yourself according to how you look, so only people who look like elevens out of ten go out with elevens and people who look like four out of ten go out with fours. He's an eleven and I'm a four but I don't care. I think, I don't care if I look like a four; you've got to work really hard if you want my attention. Which does feel empowering! I do feel like that. I'm glad I come from a very working-class background because I'm quite grounded.

Last week in the dance class I *really* felt like the artist that I am in the room but I also felt sexy and the woman that I am. Because they're combined for me. When my artist is up and I'm liking what I like and I don't like who I don't like, I feel very empowered, I'm interested in being myself. I don't want to be part of his harem. I wouldn't mind having *my* harem. If it was a woman having a whole load of guys around her I wonder what conversations women would be having about it? They have other language for that, which is, 'She's a slut, ergh!' There's something about a woman being really open, saying, 'I'm going to pick one of you tonight. And that's the deal. And none of you know which one it is. Whoever laughs hardest will get it.' That would be quite shocking, wouldn't it? My friend said about this guy with the harem, 'When we got to this dinner place, more women joined the table.' It sounded quite bizarre. I was like, 'I don't like that he's doing it, but if I was doing that, I would like it.'

Can you imagine it? You're going out for a meal with five men, and they all want to really please you and they're laughing at everything you say and then five more join and you can pick one, or none. And go, 'Well, there's five men, and there's five more coming and I don't know which one ...' Women don't imagine they can have a harem of men. Why *couldn't* a woman have a harem of men? There's something about choosing as a woman that's part of the sexual thing. When people say, 'Women get involved,' I think, 'No, actually, I could do the opposite.' There are all these precepts about how women work and there's not enough research gathered. People say things like 'Men can sleep with women and not care but women can't do that.' I think, there's a whole fucking trade of women as prostitutes, what are you talking about? When men say women aren't like that, it's a bit of a head-fuck because how come prostitution is the oldest business in the book?

I wrote this song called 'White Spider'; it's a jokey song. The end line is, 'I'm going to run naked in the wilds and I'm going to sink my teeth into your parts and into your cock, then I'm going to rip your head off when I'm done.' I do have that energy in me. Not the most romantic thing ever! Slightly praying mantis thing, and that is not something I've learned to do or be. When I'm singing that song, women *laugh* like hell. They laugh through recognition or they laugh that this little woman's going, 'I'm going to sink my teeth into your parts and into your cock then I'm going to rip your head off when I'm done.' It's the opposite of, 'Oh, a woman gets broken in sex.' I think women get fed. Often in our culture for a woman to have sex is depleting and it's taking away from her respect rather than, actually, sex makes me more of a woman, more sexy and more of who I am. I've heard friends say, 'I've got to the point now where I prefer not to have sex.' You can see there's a dullness in them. There are lots of benefits to having sex that are about our aliveness. Sex is about joy. It's about joy for women, or why else do it?

I haven't done anything with anyone for a while – and there's nothing like the real thing. Sexual fantasies tend to come to me more when I'm not being sexual. I used to have this recurring sleep dream that I was on the *Orient Express* train and I would go into a compartment and I would have great sex with a man and he would go out and I wouldn't have to speak to him. Then another man would come in and if he didn't please me I would reject him. The train was going to this destination but these men were coming in and going out and some of them I would tell to go and some of them I would allow to stay.

I've lived out quite a few of my fantasies. There was one guy – I was with another guy at the same time as him who I nearly got married to until I realised that really wasn't the right thing, I said, 'Yes' because he asked me! Anyway, that's a whole other subject. This other guy had a fantasy about having sex on public transport. I said, 'Okay, I haven't thought of that as a fantasy of mine, but I'm game.' He said, 'That's quite interesting with your Irish Catholic background – what you're meant to say is, "Don't be so ridiculous!"' One time we were on this train and there was hardly anyone on it – there was someone a few seats down – and we didn't have sex but he basically gave me an orgasm, let's put it like that. It was exciting because I had to keep quiet and there was that moment of 'Oh, is someone moving?' I don't know if they had cameras, I don't know if we were filmed. After we finished the guy got up and walked towards the toilet and we both looked very happy and I think he was thinking, 'They've definitely done something, they didn't look like that when they got on the train.' But what can you say? Can't say anything. We were fully dressed. And we were smiling. We did it loads on public transport. Not on the tube, obviously. It was passionate. He would grab me in the street and we would find somewhere really quiet and there was something dirty about it, which was appealing to me.

I once met this guy at a party and a friend of mine said, 'He's really into you.' She said, 'Just go for it.' Anyway, we went for a date and he was all those things I thought he was: he was a rich boy, lived in Notting Hill, worked in the arts world. He was Mr Perfect and he took me out for a really nice drink in Notting Hill and we went for a meal. Yawn. 'Any chance of going in the back of an alley?' I'm not saying these days I'm into the back-of-the-alley thing, but there was something really fucking boring about it. He wasn't naughty. It was a real eye-opener for me. He was so fucking boring. I can't tell you. I kept going to the loo. He did say, 'You go to the loo a lot.' I said, 'Yeah, you're really boring.' Quite outrageous, but I felt that I was supposed to be grateful that this blond Adonis, trustafarian, Notting Hill artist was interested in a number four. I sat there and thought, even if he has all the boxes ticked and I get off with him, I would die of boredom. I really got it: I would die of boredom with this man in every way. I wouldn't even be interested in being in a bedroom with this man. What people think of as romantic is really fucking dull. I remember hearing this yoga guy saying, 'Just have a good sniff of that person, literally smell them.' People forget that mating is about smell and if you don't like someone's smell, get the hell out of there: even if they've got the right job, the right place, and you're on the same pitch, you ain't going to get happy together. It's about sex, about animals; it's about smelling each other.

Later on I was with a more mature guy; there was something about him that was so attentive in an erotic way. He was a dark horse because he didn't look like someone who was erotic. Once he was in the bedroom he was quite ... he knew where to touch; I don't mean the actual acts of sex. He was the one that taught me about the back of my neck. He was drawn to touch the back of my neck and I was like, 'Ah, I'd do anything for you now!' It was just the way ... It was almost like a whisper. It wasn't like, 'Right! Let's get you in here, girl!' He was so attentive to every part of my body and I found that really erotic. He really would ask me what I wanted: 'What do you want me to do?' And I would say, 'Yep, go down on me!' I would order him and he would say, 'Oh, I don't feel like doing that,' and I was like, 'Oh well, if you don't feel like doing that you're not getting anything else. I don't want you to fuck me, I want that.' I would literally throw him on the bed and say, 'Come on, I want you to please me.' And I think he was like, 'Shit!' And that is quite scary: an under five-foot woman going, 'Right, you'd better please me or I'm going.' We used to laugh a lot when things didn't go right, and that's nice too. I was quite immature at the time. Kind of, 'Let's see what you've got, then.' I was putting him under pressure. I wasn't saying it like that, but he felt it. I had this appetite in me that I wanted satiated.

You wouldn't think it to look at him, but we were having amazing sex; I was screaming completely. There were these Turkish garages underneath his flat and he said, 'You've got to walk past all those guys afterwards.' That particular morning I walked past and they were like, 'Morning!' He wasn't ashamed of me, but a lot of men can be suppressed around that sort of thing: 'You can let me know you're enjoying it, but not too much.' I remember a guy saying that to me: 'Do you have to scream that much?' I said, 'Yeah. I do. Clearly!' There's something about really enjoying sex. In trapeze everybody calls me The Screamer – I mean, I scream all the time. There's something about the adrenaline, and the sound and the expression. It's really pleasurable and delicious when I make that sound.

I'm not going to say how old I am. In my thirties. It's been really good for me not to be with someone for a while. Now I feel ready for something, but I want that person to be the person they are and to be as honest as my ex is – even though it really hurt when we split up. But that's part of life. I feel really grateful I had that relationship with him: it was *amazing*. We had lots of trauma, and people go on about the bad parts, but the *good* parts ... more than any man I've been with, I became the woman that I am with him and he taught me about my own beauty. And my desire. My desire, what was inside me, came out with him.

Sometimes after I've had too many wanks I think, 'I'd like to do this with someone.' Yeah, I'm quite good at it, but I'd like someone to ... That's what a partner can do; they can up my game. They give me something I hadn't even thought of. People don't see relationships like that; that people can offer you something. All the different men – all the different men, wow! – I've been with have revealed something about myself that I didn't know. The best relationships, the key relationships, in my life have unlocked some other level of myself. They're literally keys, they're key relationships. I wouldn't have known other levels of myself if I hadn't met those men.

When I do the trapeze I'm standing on the platform, I'm really frightened because it's the unknown and there's this adrenaline and I get really excited and then I jump off the trapeze and I'm swinging. Suddenly I'm doing these positions and I don't know how I'm doing them. There's a love of life in it. There's a verve in it. And when I had really great sex I felt this love of life. It releases joy. Last night, when I came down the guy who was pulling the lines just could not stop laughing. He said, 'I want to give you feedback on your trapezing but I need to calm down. It's one of the funniest things I've seen.'

That's how I feel; I love life. I come from a strict Irish Catholic background, I'm a carer, but I love sex. Sex brings out what's hidden. And when I say that, I guess I'm talking about trapeze. I mean, trapeze is not all about sex, but there is some similarity: you're there, there's nothing behind you, you're about to jump off a platform, it's unknown and with someone you don't know. Sex is a massive risk and adventure because you don't know who you're going to reveal in yourself.'

202

# 23

# Womb

Helen, 36, Hampshire

*'When the man comes to you as a man, then it's beautiful'*

'When I met my husband I was deeply, deeply masculinised. My mother is a *formidable* woman, *formidable*, and a bit like Margaret Thatcher. And my father is equally as formidable. So I'd grown up in an environment where it's okay to be a man but it's not okay to be a woman; that vulnerability, that softness, the sensitivity was completely disregarded. I'd learned to be hard-edged and tough. Well, of course, coming into a relationship, who's going to be the man? It's going to be the person who stamps their feet hardest. If the woman is becoming the man, what happens to the man? In a hetero-sexual relationship there has to be the yin and yang – the man and the woman – which means the man will drop into that feminine energy and be wimpy and the woman gets away with everything and she's stamping all over him. And that was very much my experience of my early marriage. It's not satisfying for either party. Sexually I don't want a man who's acting like a woman, and he didn't want a woman who's acting like a man.

After I had my son I became postnatally depressed and it kind of ripped us apart because I stopped being the dynamic, outward woman that I am and I became this woman sleeping in the foetal position who was lost; I was just so lost. When we started to rebuild our relationships we thought, 'Oh, swinging would be good! Because it's going to add some spice into our lives.' So for two years we explored the swinging scene and there were elements of it that were *really* good fun. We were young when we got together and it helped my self-esteem that men did actually want to have sex with me when I didn't want to have sex with myself. I really liked watching my husband have sex with other women because, um, he looked really hot! So it was great. There were times if I didn't find anyone – we used to call it 'to play with' – if I didn't find anyone to play with, and *he* would be playing with someone then that could be quite painful, which I can see was coming from my wounded place. But when I was playing with someone too, then watching him was incredible: 'Oh, right, so that's how he looks. That's awesome,' and he found it the same, he thought that was great. But there was some safety in the fact that we would be in the room together. Also a lot of times it became quite self-abuse-ish because we'd go into a party with several hundred people and it was about seeing if you could fuck the best of a bad bunch. For a lot of these people the most controversial and cutting-edge thing, the most radical thing they are ever going to do, is have sex with someone else's wife. It was just a bit, 'Really?'

One thing I *do* still fantasise about was a party in Canary Wharf where it was something like a hundred people and everyone had paid an astronomical amount of money – I mean, I thought it was astronomical – £150 per person – and it was this incredible penthouse in Canary Warf, dripping money, thirtieth floor, looking out over the banks, floor-to-ceiling glass, champagne on tap, half-naked waiters and this huge sixteen-foot bed which everyone's piled up on. It was like a Roman orgy. I can't remember if we had sex with anyone else but we had sex with me up against this glass wall and as I turned round there must have been thirty people watching us. That for me is still ... That was amazing.

Now I run a Red Tent with a collective of women in Hampshire. It is very much using the menstrual cycle as a path to a woman's spirituality, creativity and her sexuality. Fascinating. Our bleed is when we're at the peak of our femininity. It is *literally* what separates us from men. When we are shunning our bleed, we are shunning our sexuality, shunning our deep power and deep wisdom. Those bloody awful tampon adverts where women go roller skating and kite surfing – I don't want to do that. It's all very masculine. I want to be quiet and calm. The more we take our attention away from our cycle, the more we start to become men. And if we are taking on more of a masculine energy, how are we going to have good sex? How are we going to be in our sexuality? I no longer see my menstrual cycle as an inconvenience. When I bleed, it's a real joy, I celebrate what my body is doing and I can really honour it. Honouring my body and what it means is transforming everything.

The history of the Red Tent is so beautiful. In biblical times when a woman was bleeding she was sent to the Red Tent. Of course, modern-day feminists would go, 'Oh, that's disgusting: she was treated as unclean.' But that's not actually what happened. Women were sent to the Red Tent so they didn't have to do the work in the village. The tribe elders would be there to look after the children, they would be doing the cooking, and the women between them would create this community. It was a time when the women talked about what was *really* happening, the issues with their husbands, the problems within the village, with their children. The men who were left would also have this time to bond with their brothers, the other men. They would do the real talking then. We've lost this time of real deep connection and communication.

There was a woman, I believe it was fifteen years ago, and she was a single mother and a chambermaid and she had no support and she'd read a book about the Red Tent and she said, 'I need this in my life. I need the support of women who usually judge me. We need to break apart this patriarchal competition and come back to this connection.' And she started the Red Tent movement in America. And it's really exciting. In America there are thousands of Red Tents. They set one day of the month when the women come together – it's not only when women are bleeding. You bring how you are; that's the beautiful thing. Oh, it's just amazing.

The structure of the Red Tent tends to be that we will have a sharing circle. This isn't tea and sympathy or Stitch 'n Bitch. It's not like that at all. When someone is talking, they communicate with real authenticity about what's going on for them, it's not just 'Oh, I'm really pissed off with my husband,' it's 'Wow, I'm feeling this really deep pain around so-and-so.' *Really* what's happening. A real passion of mine is getting under the bullshit and getting to what's really going on for people. Although if I'm honest, I usually feel a lot of resistance before I go because my work in the National Health Service is quite emotional, with a lot of holding of emotional space for my clients, so sometimes I can go, 'Oh, it's a bit like work.'

In America, because they're so popular, they have these huge Mongolian yurts: just beautiful, beautiful. Another really great place is the Goddess Temple in Glastonbury, it's *amazing* – it's the *only* consecrated female-worshipping place in Europe – it's been open for over a thousand years – to worship the female form of the goddess, which is actually how the UK was. Bridget is the goddess of England; the British Isles were called the Brigit Isles. Britannia is actually Brigit-annia, a year of Brigit. It's really fascinating.

I got into the Red Tent from mapping my cycle. This is the work of a woman called Alexandra Pope who has literally dedicated her life to investigating the menstrual cycle and what it means. Alexandra refers to the month as four weeks broken down into seasons. Day one is the first day of your bleed and that's winter – isn't it brilliant? Winter we go in really deeply. Not interested. This is not a time when I actually enjoy being with clients; it's better for me to be sat quietly doing some admin. And it's also a time of visioning and dreaming. Our dreams are a lot more lucid and woman's intuition is really heightened during her bleed. The time of the bleed is the time of the crone, of the shaman. The energy is very inward. We're not particularly giving. We're very, very wise but we have no output to get it out there. So if someone comes to us, we give them our advice – we don't care if they take it well or not.

Then we come round to spring. That's the maiden in the first period of the menarche and then she becomes the warrior so it's the time of protests, of burning bras. It's the age of fifteen, sixteen into the early twenties – yeah! She's beautiful and her energy's out there and, actually, after we've had our bleed, our energy should be 'Yes!' Spring is the quickening. We start to put in place the ideas we've had in the winter, the dreams and visions. We will be twice as creative and productive if we do our work in spring rather than in the winter. A masculine, linear, nine-to-five job and having the same output every day doesn't work for a woman. In fact, if we lived in a matriarchal society there would be three or four days a month when she's bleeding when a woman didn't turn up to work because she's going to do double what her male counterparts do on the days when she's got that spring energy. But of course we don't support and celebrate that sort of lifestyle in our society.

We then come into summer, which in terms of arche-types is the mother, so this is the time of deep sexuality, deep lushness. It's the time that we're ovulating so our energy is very outward and if we're not actually doing the fertility thing it's when we're at our most nurturing of our family and our children. We can tolerate a lot of their stuff. Because we've got the energy. I know if I work too hard during my bleed I'm exhausted come summer, I'm not lush, I'm not fertile, I'm not sexually excited.

Autumn is the time of the high priestess, of the woman who is deeply in her power, takes absolutely no shit, and that's got a very sexy feel to it. We have no tolerance in autumn, in the week before our bleed or in that age of our lives. We say it exactly how it is: all that we could put up with from our children and our men in spring and summer, we're not toler-ating that stuff now. It's when a woman is at the absolute peak of her intuition and intolerance that she needs a man who is man enough to be with her in that place – to be with her sexually, to be with her as a life partner – there's the evolved man. Most men will be like, 'Time of the month again. Oh, she's going through a phase. Oh, I can't bear it.' He will try and stop it and squash it, whereas if he can just be with it it's very illuminating.

The moment women start coming round into the autumn or the winter, patriarchal society can't cope with that. As a woman in her mid thirties, society is starting to tell me I need to be really skinny and I need to have Botox and I need to be mahogany-coloured with my fake tan. I'm getting to the point where I'm not valid in society any more. But from understanding this map of my cycle I am all for moving into the high priestess phase, and, equally, old age – why would I fear that? I'm going to be in the crone and the shaman, and it's the most revered, it's when the woman is the most wise, it's like 'How exciting!' What we are doing is relating the menstrual cycle to the life cycle of the woman. So we have a microcosm in a month, which actually reflects the macrocosm of a woman's life. It's fascinating, isn't it? It's secret knowledge.

Before I became more feminine, my sexual leaning would have been much more what I suppose men might like, much more aggressive, more pain-based, might be more anal, getting into S&M stuff. It was quite aggressive. Whereas from doing the work of dropping into the feminine – I'm not saying it's all scented candles and plinky-plonky music, how dull would that be! – but I definitely drop into a more receptive place because I can trust that my husband is going to hold the structure. The divine feminine's natural instinct is to receive. But for a modern-day woman like me who's been in the masculine it's really scary and hard to receive, because if I don't co-ordinate every second then I'm not going to be fulfilled.

Receiving is about absolutely trusting this man and that whatever he brings is coming from the right intention – whatever he does sexually is right. This is very different from being submissive because it's about knowing where my boundaries are and how to keep myself safe. It's okay to say 'no', and it doesn't mean I don't ever want it, and it's okay for the man to be able to hear that because that is tough and men tend to take that as a big sexual rejection. I can suggest stuff, it's not that I'm completely passive, it's allowing him the opportunity to step into a really masculine place and knowing whatever he brings is coming with love. Before, it would have been me constantly suggesting, or having to masturbate during sex, in case he doesn't fulfil me. It would be coming with a fearful and dominating edge. Now I can drop into 'I'm having a really great time and that might not lead to an orgasm, or it might,' which is about the feminine flow, because the feminine has no goal. It's actually not about the orgasm; it's about the connection.

It's about both of us being in our authentic energy, with my husband being fully in his masculine, and because we know, *we know* – our intuition is *so* sharp as women, particularly in our autumn and winter – when a man is coming to us to fulfil a lack in himself. Very often men come to us as little boys wanting their mummies to make it better but they've translated that as sex. Instead of coming to us with this authentic 'I feel really shit right now, I just need to be held.' Men don't often say that – they go, 'I feel bad. Sex will make me feel better. Therefore my partner can give me sex and that will make it right.' But we know that they are coming to us for something that's not authentic and it feels a bit ick. Then being able to trust that and to go, 'Actually, no. Not now.' When the man comes to you as a man, then it's beautiful; it doesn't matter if it's ten-hour Tantric sex with candles, the right music, beautiful lighting and drapes, or if it's a quickie over the kitchen table: it's not about the sex, it's about the connection. It's not about technique; it's being really centred in your energy as a woman. Scented candles, aromatherapy oil: it's all such bollocks.

The other thing that I've learned is that there is a difference between the masculine and feminine orgasm. Men have one orgasm; they have their ejaculation. But a woman has different types of orgasm, so she has her clitoral orgasms from stimulating her clitoris, and that's well documented. Actually that's the first stage of orgasm. According to the Tantric model, if we don't go for that quick release, which is very masculine, then the second gateway can open which is the G-spot. Very often the G-spot only opens when you're at a certain level of arousal – that's why you can't find the G-spot: because you're not aroused enough. But even the G-spot is a gateway, and when it has had a certain level of arousal then the cervix opens and this can almost be painful. This is when a woman is fully ready for sex: 'Yes. I'm ready for sex now.' That's the 'Yes.' It's the opening of the cervix. So the cervical opening is a form of orgasm. If we think about it logically it makes it easier for the sperm to enter the cervix and make the woman pregnant. In the fourth stage the womb will actually start contracting.

It's not about the goal of going, 'I must have a womb orgasm.' In my experience, you can't really plan it. It sometimes happens, sometimes doesn't. Most women can find a way to have a clitoral orgasm but the other orgasms; they're pretty elusive. It takes a lot of trust and being very clear when you're in a 'yes' or a 'no' before you have sex – and that's about having a real deep connection with our bodies and with our vaginas. Ultimately it's not us saying 'yes' to sex, it's our vagina and our cervix saying 'yes'. And really having that connection to go, 'Now, yeah, this is now, I'm ready.' And having a man who's hearing when you're not ready: 'Nope! Nope!' Even if they're on the brink. This is really radical: is it okay in a relationship – even if he's started to penetrate you

– to say 'no'? Is that okay? Of course it's okay. But if you ask most women they go, 'Oh no, no, no, I couldn't do that; he'd get upset.'

There's a very beautiful Tantric exercise where, for an hour, the woman asks for whatever she wants: she asks and asks and asks. When I had to ask, wow! I really struggled with that, like I didn't know what to ask for. It's taken a long time to be able to know what to ask for. The female wound is so deep from being subjected, from being controlled, from having sex forced upon the female. Britain was a real hub for witch-hunts, for the wise women, for the feminine wound. Up until 1976 you were technically allowed to rape your wife in marriage – it wasn't illegal. It wasn't a crime. We've got this buried so deeply in our feminine psyche. It's about healing the feminine wound and women rebuilding their self-esteem as a collective.

The way I used to get off was the fantasy of my favourite film star, my favourite porn scene. I used to love porn. I would be running the images through in my head – and I know I'm not alone. I can honestly say that never happens now, it never needs to happen because sex has no beginning and no end for me any more. It certainly doesn't finish or end with my husband's orgasm, because sometimes if I'm done, I'm done and if he's not we don't continue having sex. When I come, it's finished. And I might not even come because there's no goal, and I just go, 'Yeah, that was nice, nice connection, I'm done now, thank you.' Then he can – you know – finish. Or he might go, 'Yeah, I'm finished too, I don't need to orgasm.' So the fantasy aspect for me changed and what I now picture isn't the movies running in my head, it's more about the connection. Does that make sense? So, yeah, it does really change sexually if you start connecting totally to your cycle, connecting totally to your vagina, connecting totally to your womb. It radically changes, because it stops being about the fantasy and more about the reality of what's going on. I wouldn't have my own separate fantasy life, not any more. That's because of the connection.

Our sex life is amazing. It's ridiculous. I mean, we've been together fourteen years and we're like a pair of teenagers: it's utterly crazy. Because we can't keep our hands off each other, we can have sex at all sorts of times of day. Oh God, yesterday we were sat in the lounge watching some telly about eleven o'clock in the morning thinking, 'We must go out and do some gardening', and we went, 'Right, we're going to do some gardening.' Then the next thing we know we're having sex on the lounge floor going, 'Oh, right, we didn't do any gardening!'

My relationship with my husband has got better. It's amazing. Amazing. Oh, we've got stronger, definitely, in our ability to communicate our vulnerability and our fears. The reality is we all want our life partner to think we're the best thing since sliced bread. It's very hard to show our deep, deep fear, our deep vulnerability, our deep need, but ultimately when we do there's strength and beauty in that because we're giving them an opportunity to love us as we really are and not for who they think we are, which adds to the connection, which then further takes away from the fantasy.

In fact, my husband and I have been together fourteen years, been married twelve, and we only took a vow of monogamy three years ago so this was a long journey for us. We had different vows – we couldn't really promise monogamy, I didn't know what life was going to throw at us so we've only recently said, 'Yes, we've been married ten years, it's okay. I think we can go monogamous now!'

The whole thing of women with fake tan and fake nails and fake hair and fake breasts – it's all fake. I wonder how the fake women have sex; they must have fake orgasm. They are faking what they want, faking their experience, and I don't think they are doing it intentionally. Their whole lives are becoming so fake, how can their connection be real? How can it? There are now beauty salons where you can have a vajazzle. They wax you off completely and instead of your pubic hair you have diamante crystals, these little vajazzles. You stick them where your pubic hair was. It's just odd. Do you really think Emily Pankhurst chained herself to railings to give women the vote, for women to be doing this to themselves a hundred years later? I mean, really? Is that what the suffragettes went through for us to be asserting our rights? And what about the men that think that's normal? It's so frightening from the perspective of fulfilling, nourishing sex – there's the deep fantasy! Wow! I want connected, mind-blowing sex! Wow! How are we going to do that if we're being fake? And I *don't* mean people have to go the same way as me or some of my friends with full body hair and little make-up, but there has to be a middle ground where it's not about the fake, where it comes back to what is beautiful because, actually, all men, all women, *all* women are beautiful. '

# 24

# War

Mary, 94, Norfolk

*'I was an absolute trollop when I was a Land Girl'*

'Well, I'm ninety-four years old. I've had an extremely interesting life. My life started as a second daughter of a middle-class family with a very conventional, proper upbringing. No sex education – no one formally taught me. I can remember at nineteen working in the bank, all very proper, and I met a man and he realised I was entirely innocent of any knowledge about sex and I was just an opportunity to him, I think. My mother made my father see the man at the office – it was all very Victorian – and my father said he had no business to see his daughter. It was all because of this book about sex which he'd given me to inform me. I believe I've still got it in the attic.

Once I got away from home I became a lot less proper. My opportunity to get away was when the war broke out. As I'd always been a rather outdoor person I chose to enrol in the

Land Army and I was a timber measurer. I was in woods near Little Gidding, and with three weeks' training I was deemed to be knowledgeable enough to be able to say, 'Oh, that tree will do for a telegraph pole!' Anyway it was telegraph poles and pit props and railway sleepers which were wooden in those days.

Met, most interestingly, some men in the woods. Fairground people weren't able to work because it was the blackout so the huge steam engines used to drive the roundabouts were used in the woods to haul timber. I met these very interesting fairground people. Bill and Ben were two of them, they couldn't read or write; only Wogin, the owner of the steam engines, was literate but they were all a lovely bunch. Wogin's wife had got a pair of blue kid leather jodhpurs, which she wanted to sell, and I was invited into her beautiful little caravan to try these on. The caravan was full of decorative stuff like teapots. Occasionally I used to go out and have a drink with Bill. I can remember going out once – I hadn't really learned to drink – and getting impossibly drunk and Bill, who by then was making advances towards me, was slightly put off because I was violently sick. He was very good; he rubbed my back when I said suddenly I wasn't feeling very well. That was an understatement actually.

We were delegated to the forest in pairs, so a friend came with me. She didn't actually like her billet so she stayed in a hayloft in a barn in the village. She had a chap – quite well known actually – and she used to go and see him. She was very attractive and much more controlled than I was. She didn't ... No, she wasn't like me at all. I didn't even think about getting married.

But as regards sexual experiences on the whole, I was an absolute trollop when I was a Land Girl. No, I wasn't sleeping the night with them; it was more roadside sex! Can't remember with whom now. Just one-off, out of the pub. I'd possibly meet them in the pub, then have sex at the side of the road. I didn't know them. I was up for it. Didn't bother with contraceptive, didn't get pregnant. Dead lucky. I suppose I took appalling risks really.

Well, the big problem was I was in woods near Holkham Hall and it was 1942, the invasion of Dunkirk, and all the assembled troops were encamped overnight nearby, Americans, and Canadians. Say no more. The only one I remember particularly was on the side of the main road actually, and I realised to my horror afterwards that he'd stolen my knickers and they'd got my nametag in them because they were from my boarding school!

I straightforwardly enjoyed it. Didn't bother me really that I wasn't married to them. I just had sex. I think back and think, 'Oh, that was fun!' Well, it's a lovely stimulated feeling. Orgasm in my opinion is a rare occurrence. You have sex, you enjoy it, but only occasionally does someone get an orgasm. Not so often as a man does, you see. Possibly I didn't have orgasms much, really. Possibly I did when I was having roadside sex, I don't know; I enjoyed it so I probably was. And I thoroughly enjoyed the war. Thoroughly. I was completely ignorant of it. I mean, goddamn ignorant. I remember going home to visit my parents on the train the day after Dunkirk and the soldiers were in the carriage with me, dishevelled, half their uniforms gone; I just wasn't interested. I wasn't interested in the war.

And the woods were where I met my husband, Wallace. He was one of the men who came into the wood with a horse to pull timber. His father rented a farm from the village squire. A very feudal village. His name was Squire Elliot and he was held almost with reverence. The village people didn't – wouldn't

– speak to him if he was out in the village. There was no reason why they shouldn't; in fact he was a very shy man. He used to do watercolouring. Now, I being an awkward cuss, I didn't want to have the window frames and the door of my rented cottage painted the same colour as everybody else's. Well, for that, I had to ask the squire. He said, 'You can paint it what colour you like!'

When I married my husband, it was in a tiny little village and they were all very gossipy because we used to walk around the village hand in hand before we were married. So when we got married they expected me to produce a baby within three months. That didn't happen because we'd been much more careful! That was in 1945. Margaret was born in '47, and Janet in '49. The cottage we lived in in the village had no mod cons. Oil lamps and candles. Bucket loo down the garden. No water. I had a sink but no tap over it and the water would drain into a bucket underneath.

Oh yes, yes, I was happily married. Got a bit boring sometimes, but yes. Being interested in natural history and living on a farm, there was nothing I could have wanted better. We were growing potatoes, and potato picking – backbreaking work – but I loved it. I was in love. And love surmounts every-thing. Probably we had nothing particularly in common. He was much brighter than me, especially mathematically. I've got a picture of him on the sideboard. He doesn't look like a farmer.

Then in 1984, completely suddenly, in bed beside me, Wallace died. He'd just become sixty-five. I mean, I couldn't believe he was dead by me, in bed on a Sunday morning! He had said, 'Oh, I don't feel very well,' and staggered off to the loo and then he came back and I thought, well, he's probably feeling sick, so I got a bowl and he laid on his back and held my hand and suddenly his hand released tension. I turned over and realised he'd stopped breathing and so I started giving him the kiss of life and I thought, this is silly. I realised, he's dead. What's more, if I did eventually bring him round he'd probably be brain-damaged so I stopped. I then rang my daughter next door. Sounds silly but I said, 'I think your father just died.' She came racing across and sat on the side of the bed. Well, obviously, so unexpected to be widowed, it was a total shock. But I was determined not to let grieving spoil my memories. I said, 'I've got to concentrate on all the happy memories, of which there are many.' And I think I achieved that actually. It was after I was widowed I took up pottery.

I've had a boyfriend, Eustace. He died recently; he was ninety. Jewish. Lost his parents in the Holocaust. I'd known him all his life and it only happened after his wife died. He and his wife used to come here regularly for lunch and sometimes they'd stay overnight and he continued doing that after his wife died. He was going to stay one night. I said, 'Oh dear, I've forgotten to put the electric blanket on your bed.' He said, 'Well, it's a pity to warm up two beds, isn't it?' Now this man is in his eighties, I think I probably blushed! I don't do blushing really. But I agreed. And so, yes, it went on from there.

It was an intimate relationship with Eustace but more cuddles. But no, sex is not part of my life any more. Some people, I do think, have sex in their nineties; some need it and want it. But not many. I don't think men in their nineties can get an erection. Well, some take Viagra. I don't think many women want it. It would become mentally and literally a bit of a pain. I have never indulged in self-satisfaction at all, never ever. But my last chap, Eustace, he mentioned it to me because he said his wife did it and I said, 'Well I ... ' He said, 'You must have! All women do.' 'No.' Well, no, I didn't and that's it. No need. I never think about whether I'm sexually satisfied. My sexuality changed over time. I have less need of it. I'm less responsive to it. Sometimes I didn't particularly – I'm referring to in marriage – want it, but I did it to oblige. That was my role as a wife; it was something my husband wanted.

I have an appalling tendency to think I can get away with saying anything to anybody because I'm ninety-four. The trouble with being ninety-four, you lose so many of your contemporaries. I've got one close friend who's ninety, Audrey, we argue all the time, but she's a close friend who lives nearby. I've led a fairly sensible farmer's wife existence but it's all to do with genes. I'm not frail. I eat like a horse. I'm too fat. I'm told I've got a voice like a foghorn. I'm so lucky: I'm a bit deaf, not profoundly deaf, but otherwise, I still drive, thank goodness. My licence has just been renewed. Oh yes, I'm into life. I am. I am. I don't think about dying. And I'm not religious. I'm not ready to die; I've got so much more life to live, so much more I want to experience.

It was only six weeks ago that I broke my hip. I broke it outside the blacksmith's back door because I'd had Sally, my labrador, put to sleep the day before. The blacksmith, who's become a great friend, was also very fond of Sally, and I was feeling bloody miserable, shedding tears, and I thought, 'Oh I'm going to go round and have a word with Chris.' I just fell down. Outside his door. And he was wonderful. He got the ambulance, he rang my daughter, came to see me in hospital, popped round afterwards. A great friend. And, yes, a real artist. He makes *amazing* sculptures and he only started doing it when he was forty-five. He's in his forties. He's got one problem – verbal diarrhoea. I now say, 'Oh, shut up Chris,' and walk away. Yes, I'm very fond of him. He could be my next boyfriend. Well, yes.'

# Acknowledgements

Thank you to the people who were early readers and gave me advice, some of whom have been asked to be left out of the acknowledgements but nevertheless made very valuable contributions. Thank you to Adrian Cross, Anita Patel, Barrie Musgrave, Ben P., Bernadine Evaristo, Blake Morrison, Celia Michaels, Charlotte Tarrant, Dianne Benham, Emily Hayward Whitlock, Flo Hanson, Flo Perry, Frances Nutt, Freed of London, Gaelle Lemoine, Gina Langton-Durkin, Grayson Perry, Harriet Winterburn, Helen Fox, Henrietta Colvin, Jemima Jabb, Jeremy Knight, Jewels Wingfield, Jo Hislop, Kate McGeever, Kristen Palazzo, Laura Edwards, Libby Nehill, Linden Hibbert, Livia Franchini, Louise Botos, Luisa Richards, Mark Benham, Martyn Eagles, Mary Beard, Mary Mike, Matilda Aspinall, Natalie Dorchester, Neil Shashoua, Nick Barlay, Nicky Forsyth, Nicole van Zomeren, Nina Stibbe, Paula Nightingale, Pete Ayrton, Peter Ayton, Peter Robinson & the Bradshaw Foundation, Phyllis Richardson, Rebecca Egan, Sally Woodward Gentle, Sandra Newman, Seraphima

Kennedy, Simona Valeriani, Sophie Molins, Susie Boyt, The Cinema Museum, Verity Woolf, Xinran, Zoe Pilger. And to the women I met in the Forest of Dean – thank you!

Particular thanks to Helen Arthur for intelligent support, Sally Furnival for listening when the book was only an idea, Nell Leyshon for encouragement and spot-on feedback, and Kent Carroll for advice and belief.

Thank you to my agents, Jenny Hewson, Peter Straus and Matthew Turner at Rogers, Coleridge & White for understanding contracts, advising me well, and having cracking parties. Thank you to my editor, Hannah Westland, for immediately understanding what I was trying to do, for considered and intelligent editing, and exceptional patience and kindness.

I'd also like to thank George Frankl, Lila Berg, Lorna Sage and Rachel Pinney, my wise and once fierce teachers. Thank you to Julie and Colin. And to Gwyn. And I'd like to thank a certain unnamed person who regularly declares, 'S.e.x. is gross.' I'd particularly like to thank him for not showing a blind bit of interest in what I've been writing, not drawing on the manuscript and, so long as he was reading the *Beano* or listening to books on CD and had something nice to eat, was, sometimes – on occasion – actually quiet for long enough for me to do some work.

To the women I interviewed, who remain nameless, and who entrusted me with their histories and their vulnerability – thank you.